D0198614

TRANSFORMATIONAL LIFE COACHING

Other books by Chérie Carter-Scott, Ph.D.

If Life Is a Game, These Are the Rules

If Love Is a Game, These Are the Rules

If Success Is a Game, These Are the Rules

If High School Is a Game, Here's How to Break the Rules: A Cutting Edge Guide to Becoming Yourself

The Gift of Motherhood: Ten Truths for Every Mother

Negaholics: How to Overcome Negativity and Turn Your Life Around

The Corporate Negaholic: How to Deal Successfully with Negative Colleagues, Managers, and Corporations

The New Species: A Vision of the Evolution of the Human Being

The Inner View: A Woman's Daily Journal

Baby Boomer's Bible to Life After 50

The Art of Giving: How to Bring More Joy and Pleasure into the Lives of Those You Love

Blij met Mij (in Dutch only)

Transformational Life Coaching

Creating Limitless Opportunities for Yourself and Others

Chérie Carter-Scott, Ph.D.

#1 bestselling author of *If Life Is a Game, These Are the Rules*

Lynn U. Stewart

Health Communications, Inc.
Deerfield Beach, Florida

www.hcibooks.com

Library of Congress Cataloging-in-Publication Data

Carter-Scott, Chérie.
    Transformational life coaching / Chérie Carter-Scott and Lynn U. Stewart ; with
foreword by Ric Giardina.
        p. cm.
    Includes index.
    ISBN-13: 978-0-7573-0689-1 (trade paper)
    ISBN-10: 0-7573-0689-6 (trade paper)
    1. Personal coaching.   2. Personal coaching—Practice.   I. Stewart, Lynn U.   II. Title.
BF637.P36C37 2007
158'.3—dc22
                                                                        2007032438

© 2007 Chérie Carter-Scott and Lynn U. Stewart

All rights reserved. Printed in the United States of America. No part of this publica-
tion may be reproduced, stored in a retrieval system or transmitted in any form or
by any means, electronic, mechanical, photocopying, recording, or otherwise, without the written permission of the publisher.

HCI, its logos and marks are trademarks of Health Communications, Inc.

Publisher: Health Communications, Inc.
              3201 S.W. 15th Street
              Deerfield Beach, FL 33442-8190

Cover photo by Cameron Studio
Cover design by Larissa Hise Henoch
Inside book design and formatting by Dawn Von Strolley Grove

To all of our clients, students, readers, and friends
around the world who have entrusted us with their personal
development and training over the past three decades;
to all of our MMS certified coaches who have taken
the work to their different corners of the world and
brought the light of possibility to those who had given up hope.

Contents

Foreword

When we take the time to look, we usually find someone in our past who has had a profound and positive effect on the course we set for ourselves for the rest of our lives. Usually we see it clearly only from the future that person actually helped to create; sometimes we're lucky enough—or perhaps awake enough—to recognize that person for who they are and what they are giving us while it is happening.

For me, that someone is Chérie Carter-Scott. And I was very lucky, indeed.

I met Chérie in May 1978. She was facilitating a full-day time-management workshop offered through her company, Motivation Management Service (MMS). I had been urged to take the workshop by my partner in the law firm we were putting together at the time on Union Street in San Francisco. She had already attended it herself and thought it would be of value to me. MMS was directly across the street from our law offices.

Even in the list-populated, task-filled, paper-intensive, pre-computer, and pre-PDA world of a 1970s time-management program, Chérie's open and caring heart shone through. More than that, I saw she was somehow able to focus and direct that loving energy to assist others in solving their own issues. It all resonated with something deep within me.

Within days of the completion of that time-management program, I registered for the MMS Inner Negotiation Workshop, in which I cut years off my recovery time from the perceived hurts of my childhood. Within weeks of completing that workshop, I registered for the three-month

MMS Coach Training (CT) intensive. Within months of completing the CT, I left my law firm, carried my boxes across the street, and joined the staff of MMS, where for several years Dr. Chérie and Lynn Stewart taught this often-very-much-in-his-head young man how to move his center to his heart and do his work—whatever it was—from that place.

And indeed, they taught me well, for I have successfully carried Dr. Chérie's heart-centered, trust-yourself-to-have-your-own-answers, trust-others-to-have-*their*-answers approach into several successful careers that have spanned the military, law, government, high technology, and my own consulting and coaching business.

And at the root of it all has been the MMS coaching technique.

Here at last, in the words of the founder not only of MMS, but also of the entire coaching industry as we know it, are those very same techniques that she and Lynn have shared with thousands of MMS Certified Coaches around the world.

There are not enough words to describe how pleased I am that this book exists, how honored I feel to have been asked to write its Foreword, and how delighted I am that it is now in your hands.

Ric Giardina, MMS Certified Coach (1978),
President and Creative Director, The Spirit Employed Company,
Author of *Your Authentic Self: Be Yourself at Work*

❧

Dr. Cherie Carter-Scott and Lynn Stewart are profound and wonderful gifts to the coaching world. My experience with these brilliant women dates back to the early 1980's. I will never forget my first Self-Esteem Workshop and the glorious healing breakthroughs I was given in such a loving, supportive environment.

I was hooked. I wanted to be a coach and help people get past their emotional barriers. I spent many hours with Dr. Cherie and Lynn, learning, growing, and developing coaching skills. I fondly reminisce about the magical days of my Coach Training in Aspen. It was three months of intense challenge, incredible fun with kindred spirits, and mystical break-throughs I will forever cherish.

Lynn facilitated most of my training and quickly became my coaching hero. Watching her in action hour after hour as she tirelessly, creatively, and lovingly helped people find their way to break through remains an inspiration and focus of my life to this day.

My MMS diploma is proudly displayed on the wall of my office. It is a reminder of the priceless time I was able to share with Dr. Cherie and Lynn.

That time and training turned out to be a major turning point in my life and one of my greatest blessings.

You will find this book to be a leading-edge manual of the most effec-tive coaching techniques available today. The information being pre-sented is the result of spending thousands of hours with real people dealing with real issues. This is not theory or a collection of "good ideas" about what should work. It *is* what works.

As you read this account of thirty-three years of pioneering coaching genius, don't be surprised if you find yourself being able to do things you never thought you could do. That's what happens when you spend time in the commanding yet nurturing presence of these great women. Fasten your seat-belt!

Sid Walker, MMS Certified Coach (1982)
Specializing in Sales Performance Coaching
Author of *Trust Your Gut* and *How to Double Your Sales*
by Asking a Few More Questions.

Acknowledgments

Acknowledgments

We would like to thank all those "ambassadors" who give relentless hours of dedication and service to the MMS work around the globe and to all of those who were in the first MMS Coach's Training in 1975 in San Francisco who believed in us when there was no reason to, who knew intuitively that something was "right" and wanted to be a part of drawing out another's truth: Diana Bober, Jan Martin Brady, John Collins, Sandy Ford, Addy Helbig, Jean Jones, David Manley, Katherine Martin, Carol McCartney, Lynne Whiteley Novy, Barbra Rasmussen, Franc Sloan, B. J. Snowden and Christine Stockton. Without their unwavering commitment, the work would not have been possible. To Peter Vegso and Michele Matrisciani, who believed in this book and made it available for the world to read. To Michael Pomije and Isabella, my angel, whose unwavering support on a daily basis inspires us to be the best coaches we can be! And to those who live these principles in their work and daily lives . . .

Barbara Adamich
Robert Adamich
Nader Ahmed
Krita Alshouse
Britt Andriatta, Ph.D.
Billy Joe Arthur
Erica Ashforth
Paulien Assink
Patty Aubery
Tracey Baez
Han Bak
Dave Ballantyne
David Barker
Suparna Basha
Pam Beckerman
Ger Bemer
Charlotte Bertrand
Sonja Bettendorf
Els Boonon
Sister Christine Bowman
Magdalena Brandon
Pat Browzowski
Bart Budding
Peppy Caccavale
Christina Campbell
Jack Canfield
Barbara Carton-Ryker
Misty Chadwick
Fred Chase
Tim Chedester
Remco Classen
Carol Costello
Sue Creager-Rieke
Johannes Crol
Karen Daleboudt
Yvette De Beer
Mirjam De Bruijn
Rien De Vries
Sandy Defazio
Brian DiBiaso
Renee DiBiaso
Henk Dijkstra
Marinus Ditzel
Peter Draaisma
Dianne Dreyfus
Fons Driessen
Gijs Dullaert
Suzie Eastman
David Eddes
Antoine Endtz
Theresa Enyedi

Sonja Evenson-Bettendorf
Marta Flax
Steve Flax
Sharon Fleming
Marius Frank
Stacy Frank
Connie Fueyo
Bob Furstenau
Ric Gardinia
Jeff Garnes
Robert Gersten
Ric Giardina
Kip Glover
Betty Goggia
Jacqueline Goodman
Frans Gosses
Donna Gould
Shelley Greenbaum
Hein Griffioen
Hein Gubbels
Craig Guderian
Jo-Anne Guderian
Serena Haenen
Annemiek Hagens
Bob & Molly Hamrick
Eleanor Hardy
Gordie Hardy
Patty Harpenau
Corinne Heijn
Stephen Hodes
Christine Louise Hohlbaum
Vinnie Hojecki
Steve Hoopes
Daniel Mulock Houwer
Joy Huntsman
Peter Idenburg
Jeff Jacobi
Alberto Jauregui
Shannon Jauregui
Denise Johnson
Carol Jones
Judylynn Jones
David Jordan
Shaylene Kauver
David Keller
Kirtus Kimball
Elizabethe Kleinveld
Stacey Knight
Dieter Konig
Katrinka Kramer
Lori Leighty

Jeff Leith
Monica Lenches
De Ann Letourneau
Jeff Link
Marilyn Louden
Eva Love
Suzette Magiore
Jan Martin
Kate Martin
Anne Marie McCarrie
Tracy McMillan
Patty Michaels
Bill Milham
Rob Mommers
Rob Mudda
Sarah Nichols
Karel Noordzij
Sophie Noordzij
Will Noyes
Lynn Oker
Freek Ossel
Bruce Pace
Andrea Papalexatos
Katherine Peck
Dimphy Peters
Anies Phigeland
Christine Philips
Frits Philips
Els Philips-van Slingelandt
Barbara Piper
Michael A. Pomije
Ton Pover
Suzie Prudden
Karla Rehm
Marlane Ricks
Dorothy Roberts
Jac Rogen
Tijs Rokers
Carol Rosenberg
Judy Rossiter
Regina Ruff
Daan Ruud
Michael Scar
Johan Schaberg
Linda Scharf
Harry Schmalz
Jamie Schmalz
Lorraine Serena
Kathy Shannon
Alberto Simonitto
Roland Slot

Nicoline Smoor
Sara Spataro
Harry Starren
Sudi Staub
Bob Steevensz
Kathy Steinke
Joya Stoutjesdijk
Marieke Strobbe
Judith Sussman
Thom Suzawith
Linda Tappeiner
Marijkel ter Haar
Pieter ter Haar
Rob ter Haar
Susie Thomason

Joy Uppelschoten
Ben van Baaren
Dicky van den Broek
Jeannette van den Ingh van
    Wijk
Esther van der Valk
Bartjeroen van der Veen
Marcel van der Velden
Tineke van der Vorst
Iris van Harren
Jan Hein van Joolen
Barbara van Laere
Nisje van Lawick
Wendy van Leusen
Ellen van Orden

Margreet van Roosmalen
Searl Vetter
Dawn Von Strolley Grove
Anke Waijers
Herman Waijers
Sid Walker
Chiyan Wang
Lisa Whitney
Maaike Wiarda
Pieter Wijffels
Candice Williams
Marianne Williamson
Sandy Wright
Kevin Young
Ron Zecher

Preface

In these complex times, we are bombarded by more stimulation than ever before in the history of the world. The stimulation comes in the form of visuals—billboards, advertising, newspapers, magazines, television, DVDs, video games, the Internet, and e-mail; and audio—random noise, music, radio, TV, cell phones, and so on. For the most part, when stimuli bombard us, the messages are to buy, do, or go somewhere. The messages tell us we would be happier and our lives would improve if we did something different from what we are currently doing. This is the reality of the twenty-first-century world in which we live, and it will only increase. In addition to the constant barrage of stimuli, we also must contend with task-saturated lives in which responses are expected in nanoseconds, and there is less and less time to process information and data. In summary, less time, higher expectations, and a plethora of visual and auditory stimulation create stress. With stress comes confusion, doubt, uncertainty, and a certain amount of anxiety. If you are juggling multiple tasks, trying to get more done than seems possible, and are faced with decisions you don't feel confident making, you are not alone. This condition has given rise to the need for coaching.

In 1974, Dr. Chérie Carter-Scott started coaching professionally, and in 1975, she designed and taught the first Motivation Management Service (MMS) Coach Training. Since then, The MMS Institute, Inc. and The MMS Worldwide Institute, BV (MMSWI) have been conducting Coach Trainings around the world.

These Coach Trainings have helped thousands of people assist others in making inner-directed choices. These choices have reduced stress and enabled people to take action, producing more satisfaction and fulfillment. Just as so many other inventions by women have been credited to their male counterparts, until recently Dr. Carter-Scott's contributions have either been unacknowledged or have been credited to others.

Now you have the opportunity to learn from the source, the person who "invented" coaching, who designed the first coach training, and who knows coaching better than anyone on the planet. Dr. Chérie's coaching approach is truly profound.

Whether you are a professional coach or you use coaching in your work with employees, patients, clients, or customers, this is the handbook you will want to always keep close by your side. Learn from Dr. Chérie, and help multitudes of people through your helpful coaching.

Lynn Stewart
CEO, The MMS Worldwide Institute, BV,
Master Coach, and Corporate Change Agent

❧

Dear Reader,

I designed the original MMS Coach Training in 1974. Lynn Stewart and I have been teaching the MMS Coach Training, and training trainers to teach our program, since 1975. Throughout the years, our students have urged us to write a book on the MMS coaching method. In the early 1970s, we were the only game in town; however, as I predicted, coaching became so popular that it has become a profession, and subsequently, many books have been written on the subject. We thought that the world didn't need one more book on coaching, but our students countered with the encouragement: "MMS coaching is special, different, and unique; your book will be different from all the others!" We finally succumbed to the many requests and wrote this book for our MMS and MMI students, and for those of you who want a handbook to become a "brilliant" coach.

If you are reading this book, you must have some interest in coaching. You may be enrolled in the MMS or MMI Coach Training, or you might be in another coach training course that uses our text, or you simply want to know everything you can about coaching. Regardless of why you are reading this book, we hope you find it to be a support for you on the path to helping others. We have found that coaching is one of the most effective ways to help people sort out their options and preferences, and to make integrated choices. Enjoy the reading, and please feel free to contact us through our website: www.themms.com, and go to www.mmsVT.com for our 24/7 Virtual Training and www.themms.eu.

Blessings on your coaching journey!

Chérie Carter-Scott, Ph.D.

The Relationship with the Self

"It is what a man thinks of himself
that really determines his fate."
Henry David Thoreau

If you aspire to become a certified coach, you must first focus on your relationship with your "self." Before coaching another, you must first be connected to yourself. You must be aware of what goes on inside of you before you can build a bridge to another. You can only ask another to do the work that you personally have done. Becoming a coach is a journey that starts with your relationship with you.

Your relationship with yourself is the central template from which your personal destiny manifests. The relationship with the self is the most important and crucial relationship in your life. Your career, your personal relationships, your home, and your health are all a direct result of the quality of your relationship with you. The way you hold yourself creates a vibration that sends a message to the world about who you are, what you deserve, and how you should be treated.

The relationship with the self is the way you hold, perceive, believe in, and relate to you. It is comprised of the various thoughts you have about yourself, the ideas you have about how others perceive you, the emotions you feel about yourself, your judgments about yourself, your perception of your self-worth, and your internal conversations in your mind. Your relationship with yourself includes the way you treat yourself, whether you abuse, neglect, or honor your needs, feelings, and wants. It also includes the promises you make to yourself, the subsequent actions that you take, and the manner in which you deal with your completed projects and your broken agreements with yourself: when things go your way, how you express your satisfaction; when things go awry, how you deal with your displeasure. If everything goes perfectly, how do you interact with you? How do you relate to yourself when circumstances occur that are disappointing, upsetting, or unfortunate? Your relationship with yourself includes how you make decisions and choices, and the manner in which you determine your life compass. Your relationship with yourself, however, goes beyond making choices, and encompasses every interaction that you have with yourself, every moment of every day. It starts when you awaken in the morning and extends to your dreams throughout the night.

In addition, this relationship includes how you relate to and manage your productivity on a daily basis, how you manage your time, energy, projects, finances, and network of associates. The essential question is: do you manage your motivation with diminishment, dismissal, and disregard, or do you use the tools of recognition, reinforcement, and reward? If you have never thought about this, consider this concept. When you are "at one" with yourself, you are in alignment, and it is peaceful inside. When something happens that does not meet your expectations, a conversation can start that splits you in two. The dialogue that ensues is between you (your public self) and the self (the private you). Or the dialogue may include more than two voices, but the point is you are no longer at one, and it is no longer quiet inside. Sometimes the voice engages when you must make a decision and are uncertain about what to do. An opportunity may be offered to take a job in a remote location away from family or friends, or you have a proposal of marriage and are uncertain whether the person you have been dating is someone with whom you want to spend your life. Whatever the situation, when the mental dialogue starts, you are no longer present, and you have become more than "one." The list on the left is the part of you that surfaces when you are alone and present. The list on the right is the part that surfaces when you split and find yourself "at odds" with yourself.

Essential self	Ego
Private self	Public self
Child	Parent
Employee	Manager

You won't necessarily relate to all of the pairs listed, but out of the four pairs, you might find one set with which you identify. Locate the pair that best fits your relationship with yourself and hold those labels in your mind as you read on.

When things don't sit right with you, you have a choice. The choice is between speaking up or remaining silent. Ignoring or pretending things are fine when they aren't only exacerbates the split between you and your authentic self. When you do what you say, and make your word count, you are operating with integrity. Integrity comes from a Latin word that means whole. Integrity means that you are undivided and adhere to your principles and standards even when it is inconvenient. When you operate with integrity, you are aligned with your highest aspirations of yourself.

Belinda, one of our coach trainees, had an addiction for chips. When she felt frustrated, she would eat a whole bag of chips, and after she finished, she would come to her senses. She would then beat herself up for indulging in the chips. Every time Belinda ate chips, it became a wedge between her essential self and her ego. She would explain, justify, and defend her need for chips, but she hated the fact that there was this schism: the part of her that wanted to stop unconsciously eating chips and the part of her that could not control herself. Chips were Belinda's way of giving herself some short-term pleasure when she felt stressed and pressed for time. When she had no time to take care of herself, she would stuff some chips into her mouth, feeling briefly relieved of the frustration; yet later, when her higher self reappeared, she felt guilty, let down, ashamed, and sad. The only way out of this "negaholic" addiction was for Belinda to start connecting with herself and feeling her feelings. When she felt frustrated, she had to start experiencing and expressing her feelings rather than stuffing them down with chips. It was because she wanted to be a brilliant coach that Belinda became strong enough to resist the urge to sneak chips and to say, "No, I won't be able to ask my clients to do what they say they want to do unless I am true to myself." Belinda reached out for support, became reconnected with herself and her feelings, and overcame her chip addiction.

You may be conscious of your relationship with yourself, or you may be unaware of it, but either way it is the most powerful connection that you have with your essential life force, your authentic self, and your core identity . . . and those are the keys to your future.

Most people are unaware that a relationship with the self exists. They simply live their lives bouncing off of other people's expectations, opinions, approval, and rejection. Without the awareness of their interior world, they do not engage in reflective moments that examine where they've been, where they are, and where they would ideally like to be. They may question, compare, idealize, blame, envy, become angry or depressed, or live vicariously. They may have dismissed the possibility of having dreams or formulating goals. They may have talked themselves out of their wishes or hopes, or they may have surrounded themselves with people who don't believe in them and consequently diminish their timid yearnings. If a person has never examined what he or she truly wants, assessed what might be in the way, and mapped out an action plan, then that person is probably disconnected from his or her essential self and unaware of the many possibilities that this core relationship can provide. The discovery of this relationship with the self illuminates new vistas for growth, self-development, and fulfillment, and opens doors that were previously closed. Your relationship with yourself is ongoing and never takes a vacation. If you are going to be a "brilliant" transformational coach, you must have a healthy and functional relationship with yourself.

THE TWO SIDES OF THE SELF

Each one of us has two distinct aspects: the "I can" side and the "I can't" side. The "I can" side is confident, competent, capable, certain, and in control. The "I can't" side is insecure, uncertain, fearful, and reactive to other people's needs, wishes, agendas, and expectations. The purpose of the "I can't" side is to keep you safe from risks and harm. The purpose of the "I can" side is to stretch you out of your comfort zone and encourage you to grow.

All of us possess both the "I can" and the "I can't" sides, but like a pie that is divided into slices, the percentage of each slice will vary from person to person and from situation to situation. What determines the percentage of "I can" versus the percentage of "I can't" is related to one's personal history, one's significant experiences, and whether the positive or negative side has been reinforced over time. For example, if a person has the ratio of 60 percent "I can't" and 40 percent "I can," the initial impulse to a new expansive opportunity will be to respond with the knee-jerk reaction of "I can't do it!" The different forms this "I can't" may take are: I can't deal with it. I can't afford it. I can't get it done. I can't learn it. I can't handle it. I have coined the word, *negaholic,* which represents the "I can't" side of the self.

On the other hand, if a person has the ratio of 60 percent "I can" and

40 percent "I can't," the initial impulse to a new situation is to respond with hopeful enthusiasm. It may sound like, "Let me do it. I'm the right person for the job." That doesn't mean that since the percentages are weighted on the "I can" side that the realization of the wish is a solid guarantee, but rather that there is less negative history in the form of old wounds, decisions, attitudes, beliefs, and self-sabotaging behaviors. With every goal, dream, or wish comes a series of challenges or obstacles. How you deal with the obstacles is what builds or erodes your relationship with yourself. Each time you overcome a challenge or obstacle or surpass your belief in what you can do, you are fortifying your self-concept and building your belief in yourself. Each time you back down from a new opportunity, you are eroding your self-concept. Each time you succumb to the belief that you can't do something that you truly want to do, you are reinforcing your lack of belief in yourself. In addition, you might start out at 70 percent in the "I can" zone professionally but come up against a huge challenge and drop to 30 percent, losing faith in your own ability to successfully deal with the situation.

Jim felt he was up to the task when his boss asked him if he could tackle the telecommunications liaison job interfacing with management, training sales, dealing with service, and handling customers. He thought, *I have done all of these functions in other jobs. I can do it.* When he was promoted, he realized he was in over his head. He felt that the job required more skills than he had. He didn't have the luxury to learn on the job, and the expectations were so beyond his reach that he had to either deliver or default. Jim had started out at 80 percent "I can," but when presented with the reality of the job, he shifted to 70 percent "I can't." Things don't stay static—they continually change. Noticing your present percentage of "I can" versus your percentage of "I can't" is a good first step in improving your relationship with self. The second step is to notice and pay attention to your mind chatter. When you have implemented those two steps, then you have the awareness to begin the journey. Perhaps you are 90 percent "I can" in your professional life and 40 percent "I can" in your personal life. You might consider having a coach to help you build the 40 percent "I can" into 80 percent.

HOW A COACH CAN HELP WITH YOUR RELATIONSHIP WITH YOU

The coaching process has three phases: (1) to clarify what you want, (2) to map out an action plan to get what you want, and (3) to support you to the realization of the vision, dream, or goal. All three phases are included in every Motivation Management Service (MMS) transformational coaching project. These phases happen in each session and are mirrored in the coaching relationship between coach and client.

In addition, three assumptions are always present in each coaching session: (1) people possess their own answers to their individual challenges; (2) people possess the personal power to make their intrinsic answers become reality; and (3) people and organizations can have their visions, dreams, and goals become reality. If these assumptions are not true for you, it is going to be a challenge to empower another. If you are to coach others, you need to believe in them. If you are to believe in them, you must first believe in you. If you have had the experience of discovering your own answers, it will be much easier to believe that others truly have their own answers inside of themselves as well. If you have been able to manifest your heart's desires, then it will be much easier for you to trust that others can manifest their visions, too. If you allow support to empower you, it will be easier for you to completely support another.

Bridging the Gap

When the stretch between where you are presently and your desired future reality is more than you can imagine, a coach helps you bridge the gap between "here" and "there." A coach helps you manage the "I can't" or the negaholism that surfaces in the form of confusion, doubt, uncertainty, and fear that can sabotage your dreams. Every time you achieve another goal, you contribute to the evolution of the self. Your identity changes each time you grow into increased dimensions of yourself.

I had been out of school and working for fifteen years when I discovered I had the desire to complete my education and get my master's degree and doctorate. The people surrounding me said, "You don't need it. You have successfully built your coaching business, and you don't need that piece of paper. You certainly don't need to spend the time, energy, and money at this phase of your life." Although what they were saying sounded correct, the urge to continue my education was persistent and wouldn't go away. I kept imagining myself researching, writing papers, and stimulating my intellect. The dilemma I faced was whether to listen to my friends and attempt to dismiss the "message," or to trust the message and apply for graduate school. My mind reminded me that no one in my family had pursued a graduate-level education. I called my own coach and asked if we could have a session on graduate school. The session allowed me to connect to my internal motivation and simultaneously assess what others were saying to me. In the session I formulated a plan to fully research the options to see if graduate school was truly my choice. I obtained a brochure that spoke to my situation, my aspirations, and to me personally. I applied, was accepted, and eight years later I graduated. It was with the support of Lynn, my coach, that I aligned my energies toward my goal and made a choice for my future. This was a specific issue that would definitely *not* leave me alone. You may have one of these secret desires that simply won't go away. How you deal with or suppress your "message" will directly influence how you deal with your client's secret wishes, desires, and messages when they surface in a session. The mirror of your own life will reflect in the way you listen to, empower, and support your client. If you are not living up to your own dreams and aspirations, it will be very difficult to support others in living up to their wishes, hopes, and passions.

Starting the Year with Focus

Each January you can meet with your coach to help you determine your goals for the year. If you don't have goals, you could easily become confused as to where to focus your energy. You might simply "go with the flow" or see what shows up in your life, but if you want to take control of your own destiny, then you have to do the work of assessing your preferences, talents, and capabilities, and formulating your goals. Once you have formulated your goals, both you and your coach can focus on what you want to achieve. If you don't know what you want, a coach can help you determine what you value, and where you want to direct your time and energy. The coaching conversation regarding values, focus, and goal setting aligns both of your energies toward the agreed-upon objective. This is a good starting place for a new coaching relationship.

Acting as a Sounding Board

A coach can also help you externalize your thoughts and feelings regarding your goals. Formulating goals is important, but stating them doesn't automatically guarantee that they will happen. It isn't like the genie from the lamp who looms up in front of you asking for your three wishes. You must focus, intend, and do whatever you need to do to make your goals become reality. Your coach will encourage you to share your secret wishes, dreams, and goals. A coach helps you to track your progress, and to recognize, reinforce, and reward the achievement of your desired outcomes. Sometimes the thoughts and feelings regarding a specific issue become jumbled in your mind. When this happens, the coach serves as an objective entity who can help you sort out the spaghetti of the mind into individual strands so that you can make choices. The definition of choice is "to select freely from a series of alternatives that which you want."

Mirroring

Your coach will also act as a mirror, enabling you to see what is evading or obscuring your view. Imagine that you are trying to cut the hair on the back of your head without a mirror. Of course, it is possible to do this, but you are unlikely to be happy with the results. Your coach enables you to see that which you may have trouble seeing on your own.

Susan, an expatriate living in Europe, was excited about her new apartment, but when she went to sign the papers, she became ambivalent because of her perfectionism, the price, and the commitment. She was derailed and about to renege on her choice because of fear. With the help of her coach, she was able to get back on her feet, remember her choice, and move forward. Her coach helped her see what she had originally wanted. The apartment was not only workable; it filled almost all the requirements on her list.

Believing in You

Another area in which your coach can be incredibly useful is in helping you to believe in yourself. Research has shown that people who believe in themselves are much more likely to make their dreams come true than those who don't. If your dream requires you to stretch your self-image, then your coach can help you find the building blocks between your current perceptions of self to your desired identity.

Henry, a director of a prominent training center, wanted to change his image from being a successful international director to being a known author, speaker, and media personality. When he started working with a coach, he altered his previous self-image and began to reinvent himself in light of his new profession. Coaching was the vehicle he used to shift to his new identity.

Getting You Back on Your Feet

A coach can also help when you encounter disappointment, disillusionment, or rejection. When your big goal seems to constantly be shut down, you're told that "you're crazy," or everyone says, "I'm not interested," your coach can either help you reframe these experiences or assist you in overcoming the objections and breaking through the blocks.

James had done everything he could imagine to manifest the life he wanted. He kept encountering rejection over and over again. He didn't know if this was a test of his commitment or a sign that he was doing the wrong thing. He kept asking himself why things weren't flowing the way he thought they should. He kept wondering if he should sell his company, get a job or hang in there through this difficult period. When James met with his coach, she helped him see what was going on from a higher perspective, recommit to his business, and formulate the tasks that would keep him focused and produce the desired results.

Facing a Crossroads

Sometimes it is difficult to sort out what direction you should take. Deciphering whether the circumstances indicate that you should abandon a project or whether the indicators are simply tests to see how much you really want something is often difficult. For instance, is the following a message or is it a test? Am I supposed to press through the obstacle, or am I supposed to cut my losses because there is no way to win in this situation? I asked my husband if he would take flying lessons with me. He declined, saying he suffered from motion sickness. So I signed up for flight school on my own. Shortly after I began, John Kennedy, Jr., died in his historic plane crash. Then, three weeks later, my flight school went out of business. I kept encountering one obstacle after another, and I started to wonder if I was really supposed to do this or if the signs were telling me that this was foolhardy. My coach helped me sort out the truth about all these events. I completed my flight training, but it wasn't without challenges. After I received my pilot's license, my husband decided to get on board and learn how to land a plane in case something unforeseen happened to me in flight. He then became inspired, got licensed to fly single-engine aircraft, and we both became instrument-rated pilots.

Holding You Accountable

You may be a very positive person who is surrounded by people who are negative or diminishing, have exceedingly high expectations, or are just plain negaholic. If you are in such a situation, you probably take your accomplishments for granted, have difficulty being acknowledged for your achievements, and may even discount, discredit, or let yourself off the hook when you don't do what you say you will do. In these circumstances, you could possibly use a person to serve as external accountability. A coach can support you in acknowledging yourself, in doing what you say you want to do, and in being resolute with the negative people around you.

Embarking on a New Chapter

What happens when you've accomplished what you set out to achieve? What would you do if your company was acquired, merged, or went public? A coach will help you acknowledge yourself, sort out your new aspirations, choose what is in your best interest, and embark on your new venture.

Roger was a key player in an IT company that was acquired in Silicon Valley because of an important software program developed by the engineers. After the merger, however, Roger and his employees felt unheard, eclipsed, and unrecognized for their contributions. With the help of an external coach, they had their spirits renewed and were able to find their place in the new organization.

Examining Unrealized Dreams

What becomes of those goals that never come to fruition? What happens to those wishes, good intentions, and secret dreams? Your coach will help you discover the lessons you can learn from those unrealized dreams so you can gain insight and grow from everything that happens to you. Why do some goals become derailed? Why do some people perpetually stay overweight? Why do others feel the frustration of never materializing the relationship they desire? Why do some stay in dead-end jobs, envying others who appear to have fulfillment and financial success? The unrealized goals can become the fodder for your personal development program. While you examine the *what*, the *why*, and the *why nots* of your specific goal, your coach supportively encourages you to look deeper to find the "real truth," and not settle for what appear to be reasons, justifications, and explanations for not getting what you said you wanted.

Stephan, a successful lawyer for the Federal government, became an attorney to make his father proud. After practicing law for many years, he felt unsatisfied. He wanted something tangible in which he could use his hands. In a coaching session, he discovered a secret dream to work with bicycles and open a shop. As a result, he chose to open his own bicycle store and service department. He became a much happier man as a result.

Giving Validation and Recognition

It is important to have at least one person who recognizes your accomplishments. Too often family and friends see you as you were in the past or as you are in the present. They see you in terms of your history, not your future. They may have difficulty expanding their viewpoint to include your development into new endeavors and capabilities. They may focus on your limitations rather than on your unlimited potential. They also may compare themselves to you and be threatened by your growth and expansion. Having a safe place to formulate and discuss your goals, to share your concerns, worries, considerations, and fears, is extremely helpful. Every time you externalize your doubts, it reduces their power over you.

Maaike had a lifelong dream to become an artist. She lived her life as a wife, mother, and office manager, but her secret dream was to support herself as an artist. With the help of her coach, Maaike enrolled in the Art Institute of Amsterdam, and after four years she fulfilled her life passion. At forty-five she started a new career painting and sculpting. Today she is exhibiting and taking assignments from all over the world. She has become a full-time artist.

Overcoming Fears

You may want to do something that is a big stretch for you, but fear may paralyze your motivation. You may be caught between the desire for the objective and the fear that is convincing you that you can't be it, do it, or have it. Your FEAR (False Evidence Appearing Real) may seize and immobilize you. A coach can help you overcome your fears and make the seemingly impossible happen. Here is a personal story from Lynn:

> *For years I had tried, unsuccessfully, to scuba dive. This year in Thailand, with the support of my coach, I tried one last time to overcome my claustrophobia, my physical limitations, and my fears. I was finally able to use the regulator and breathe underwater. After many failed attempts with the fear overtaking me, I experienced a major breakthrough. Through the encouragement of my coach, a sympathetic scuba-dive master, and the rigors of practice, I was able to overcome my fears and physical challenges. The desire to see the beauty of the underwater world prevailed over my fear of drowning. I am now a certified PADI diver.*

THE PROGRESSION OF PERSONAL DEVELOPMENT

Do you remember that person in your life who believed in you when you didn't believe in yourself? I am referring to the person who encouraged you when you wanted to give up, the person who would not stop believing in you no matter how convincing you were. It might have been a teacher, athletic coach, friend, uncle, aunt, sibling, minister, spouse, mother, or father who showed you how not to give up . . . on you. That person probably even built a case on your behalf to prove the point, and was so filled with ammunition that you may have been embarrassed or even disbelieved him or her.

Everyone who has ever achieved anything in life has had at least one person whose support was unrelenting. In the highly mobile world in which we live, it is difficult to surround yourself with people who have that unconditional commitment to your success. In large companies, it is often unsafe to communicate your aspirations, rejections, concerns, worries, fears, or even goals. Very often people are eager to use information for their own professional positioning and personal gain. Your coach, however, will be one of your greatest cheerleaders and will commit to your success no matter what.

There is a progression for each person who embarks on the self-development path. You may join at level 1, 2, 3, or 4, but the progression is the same. You will encounter five levels in your journey to growing your self. The first level is the condition called "disconnection with the self." At this level, you don't know what you want. And even if you have a faint idea of what you want, you don't believe that you could be it, do it, or have it. At the second level, you encounter the condition called "desire and defeat." At this level, you know what you want, but there is more self-doubt than confidence. The third level is called "limits to deserving." At this level, you have grown in your belief in self, but it still has limits, holding back unlimited possibilities. Level 4 is called "connection and abundance." At this level, you have broken through any limitations, and you are primed to go for everything you want. Level 5 is called "union and manifestation." At this level, you have fulfilled your heart's desire and have achieved what you set out to do. This progression emerges in every coaching relationship, since it is about the evolution of the self. The coach's primary goal is to assist in your personal evolution. The coach needs to be able to assess where you are and what will support you in getting to where you want to go. If you are the coach, you need to have first-hand experience of what each of these levels feels like.

Levels of Personal Development

Level 1: Disconnection with the Self
I don't know what I want.
I can't be it, do it, or have it.

Level 2: Desire and Defeat

I know what I want, *but* . . .

I can't be it, do it, or have it.

Level 3: Limits to Deserving

I know what I want, *and* . . .

I can have some of it (*but* not all of it).

Level 4: Connection and Abundance

I know what I want, *and* . . .

I can have it all!

Level 5: Union and Manifestation

I have what I want!

Coaching Session Objectives

If you are on the continuous improvement program, you will travel down this road many times in your life. Every time you get what you want, it ignites the motivational spark that yearns for the next adventure, mountain to climb, or personal conquest. Whether you want to start a business, become scuba certified, or drive a race car, this will be your road map. No matter at which level you begin, you must identify your areas of concern, and from that list formulate your objectives. Review the following list and see what might be your objectives.

- **Health:** This could be a health concern of yours or a concern regarding the health of a family member or friend. It could relate to any aspect of health, including but not limited to how to maintain your health; confronting health procedures that are uncomfortable yet necessary; what supplements to take; how to feed yourself, especially when you have allergies or travel often; how to maintain, increase, or reduce your weight; how to deal with a health crisis with a loved one or within yourself; or other health issues involving sleep, exercise, pain, energy, vitality, sex drive, stamina, sight, hearing, coordination, or motivation.

- **Work/career:** This could relate to solving a specific problem at your current job, a new job opportunity, getting out of a dead-end job, strategically positioning yourself for advancement, redefining your career goals, changing careers, searching for a new career, or designing life after retirement.

- **Home:** This includes formulating what you need and want in a new home, how to go about finding the perfect home for you, decorating your home on your budget, making your home the cozy "nest" that you want, relocating to another city, state, or country, redefining what you mean by home, and making the shift to include another into your home.

- **Relationships:** This includes relationships with all the significant people in your life—spouses or partners, parents, children, friends, bosses, employees, and work associates—and can address determining what you want in a relationship; finding or manifesting a new relationship; strategizing how to meet potential candidates for a relationship; working on roles and responsibilities, impasses, areas of hurt, or communication breakdowns; or how to supportively end a relationship.

- **Finances:** This includes how to control your spending, how to increase your revenues, how to live within your means, how to solve an immediate financial problem, how to exponentially increase your net worth, and how to manifest the financial success you have dreamed of.

- **Balance:** This could be how to find balance between work and leisure time, waking moments and sleep, exercise and stillness, being and doing, excitement and stress, and managing the time in your life so that you feel you are in the driver's seat.

- **Happiness:** This includes what is in the way of being happy and what needs to happen to create a happier life.

- **A stressful concern:** This is something you are wrestling with, thinking about, worried about, or are experiencing fear about. It includes addressing specific problems such as procrastination, phobias, negativity; difficulty declaring boundaries and saying "no"; and overcoming blocks to almost anything: reading, public speaking, dealing with numbers, success.

- **Inner peace:** This means finding a core inside you of peace and well-being that knows who you are, why you are here, and the purpose of your life.
- **Next phase of life:** This includes the next chapter, where you want to go from here. It may mean that you have accomplished your major goals or that you have a life-threatening condition. It may mean that your circumstances have radically changed, and you need to shift from feeling the recipient of the news to the author of the situation.

Rather than having a concern "pop up" in random situations, you take hold of the item, look it squarely in the eye, and determine what you want to do about it. Confronting what you are trying to avoid is a good use of your coaching relationship. In order to do this, you need to be aware of what you are avoiding.

Formulating Objectives

You always want to put objectives into the infinitive form of the verb. When you do this, you have forward motion and an immediate focus. You have determined what you want to get out of the session. Here are some examples:

- To overcome . . .
- To clarify . . .
- To formulate . . .
- To determine what is going on with . . .
- To manifest . . .
- To create a plan . . .

- To organize . . .
- To discover or find . . .

How to Choose a Coach

There are three steps to choosing your coach: (1) sorting out what you want from your coach, (2) interviewing various coaches, and (3) negotiating what you want, the frequency, and the cost.

Step 1: Determine What You Want in a Coach

First, you need to sort out your expectations regarding retaining a coach. Are you hiring a coach for a specific concern (for example, in the area of career, relationship, home, or health, as described earlier)? The clearer you are about your objectives, the easier it will be to choose a coach.

The most important aspect of choosing a coach is the rapport between the two of you. The connection needs to feel totally safe, as if you could say anything and would still experience unconditional acceptance. The connection with your coach must be free from judgment, and your coach must believe in you and your capabilities. Other attributes you might be interested in could be flexibility, availability, philosophy or belief system, familiarity with your situation or circumstances, gender, or age bracket.

Here are some other questions to ask yourself about your coaching preferences: Do you want this relationship to be merely one session, a series, or ongoing? Do you want to meet with your coach face to face, on the phone, or in a "chat" situation online? How often do you want to have contact with your coach: annually, biannually, quarterly, monthly, weekly, or as needed? What is your budget for your coaching sessions? Have you allocated funds for this process? Do you need to have a coach who takes insurance, credit cards, or trade outs? How do you want to pay for your sessions—in advance, pay as you go, or after they are completed? And last, how do you want to be treated? Do you want your coach to serve as external accountability, to be an expert in a specific area, to challenge your aspirations, or to provide you with unconditional acceptance at all times?

Step 2: Interview Coaches

Ask people you know who are being coached or who know coaches for referrals. You might also consider coaching associations, checking on websites of coaching groups you feel a kinship with, or even the Yellow Pages. You may want to look for referrals for coaches in a specific geographical area that is near your home or office, or for coaches who have developed expertise in a specialty area, or those in the price range you can afford.

Before you make contact, take a sheet of paper and write out what you are looking for in a coach, as you determined in step 1. After you have reviewed your profile of the perfect coach for you, the next step is to write down the questions that you want to ask each prospective coach. Here are some sample questions to get you started:

1. How long have you been coaching?
2. What method do you ascribe to?
3. Do you have a specific philosophy or belief system?
4. What approach do you use?
5. What are your coaching assumptions?
6. What are your credentials?
7. Do you have a website, or have you published anything?
8. Are there agreements that you require?
9. What happens if I break an agreement?
10. What happens if I don't achieve my goals?
11. How long is a session?
12. Do you bill by the session or the hour?
13. Who trained you?
14. How many clients do you work with at one time?
15. Do you do phone sessions, face to face, or online chat?
16. Do you assign homework between sessions?

17. What are your expectations of your client?

18. What can your client expect from you?

19. What do you charge? Do you do a series of sessions?

20. Do you take credit cards?

21. Do you take insurance?

22. Do you have a specialty?

23. Can your client speak to other satisfied clients?

24. Do you have availability in the morning, afternoon, or evenings?

25. On what days do you see coaching clients?

Gather the list of coaches with the contact information and initiate contact either by e-mail or phone. Type out all of the questions and make a copy for each coach you will interview. Write the coach's name and contact information on the top of the page so that when you make contact, you can document the phone call. If the coach prefers e-mail, then you can copy and paste the questions you have for the coach.

Step 3: Negotiate

After you have completed your data gathering, start the process of elimination. This means that you start to cull your list either by objective criteria (such as geographically undesirable) or subjective assessment (you didn't like the tone of voice). When you get your list down to either two or three coaches, take a highlighter and highlight the points you want to negotiate. Then your second set of calls or e-mails will start with you asking for what you want. For instance, if the prospective coach conducts sixty-minute sessions and you want fifteen-minute sessions instead, ask for what you want. You will find out if the connection and flexibility match with your personality and your expectations. You want this relationship to start out on the right foot, and you want to be able to ask and say anything to your coach. At the end of this process, you will have determined who your coach will be, and he or she will be compatible with your style, meet your expectations, and satisfy most if not all of your criteria. When someone is considering you as a possible coach for him- or herself, you can propose the same process. If it works with you, chances are it will work with your clients, too.

THE CHALLENGE OF COMMITMENT

If you are embarking on the journey to being trained as a coach, then your commitment to your goal will be challenged. Commitment is the act of devoting oneself unreservedly to something, someone, or some ideal—the state of being bound intellectually or emotionally to a course of action.

You must know what you want in order to choose. After you choose, then commitment is your declaration to the world that you are going to cause your choice to happen. Commitment is a declaration of intention. It anchors choice and puts a motor behind it. Commitment makes choice real.

Commitment means that you are taking yourself seriously. It means that you believe you can be trusted to cause something to happen in the world. It means that you will do what you say you will do, no matter what the obstacles. You can commit to anything: a person, a job, losing ten pounds, a belief system, a way of life, or what you want to do this weekend. It doesn't matter what you commit to; what matters is the reinforcement of your relationship with yourself based upon self-respect, self-trust, and credibility.

Commitment means putting all of your resources behind that which you have chosen. It means no holding back, no waiting to see if something or someone better will come along. It means no more whining or complaining about the obstacles. It means no more waiting for someone else to do it for you. Commitment is not passive, complacent, or hopeful. It is active and determined. It means getting out and making it happen. It means putting 100 percent of you on the line and going for what you want. When you are truly committed, nothing will get in your way: no reason or excuse can stop you.

When you are committed to someone or something, there is no more doubt or confusion. <u>You have direction, focus, and purpose.</u> Commitment enables you to have freedom and power. Commitment means you back yourself 100 percent. It means you stand behind your choices unwaveringly. <u>Commitment means claiming your power to manifest what you want in your life.</u> Commitment ultimately means being totally committed to you.

❧

Your relationship with yourself is the starting point in the self-development journey. Once you connect with yourself, sort out who you are, and determine that you want something different from what you have, you may want to consider having a coach to keep you focused on your goals. A coach can have many capabilities, but the most important aspect of a coach is that he or she truly believes in you, even when you have stopped believing in yourself.

$\mathcal{A}$wareness

"You cannot teach a man anything. You can only help
him find it within himself."

Galileo Galilei

$\mathcal{A}$ll change starts with awareness. If you are not aware, you can't
make choices, and therefore, you can't change anything. Once
you are aware of something, you have the option to change it. As
humans, we operate from habit, and when behaviors become habitual, *automatic*
we relinquish our right to choose. Awareness means that you are connected with yourself. It is the art of being fully present in the moment.
When you are aware, you pay full attention to what is happening, and
you're mindful of what is going on both within you and around you. To
the degree that you are connected to yourself, noticing what you want,
allowing yourself to have what you want, and going for what you want,
you will be the perfect "mirror," encouraging your clients to go for what
they want, too. You are free and available to notice what is happening in

the environment and with the coaching client, the "coachee," sitting directly across from you.

When you coach others, you ask about their wishes, goals, and objectives. You are interested in their desired future, and because you are drawing out their secret truths, you will help them build the bridge between where they are presently and where they want to be. This involves change. The coaching process invites change.

CLEANING THE VESSEL

In order to be fully aware, you must first "clean the vessel." Cleaning the vessel means readying yourself to be totally present and available for your coaching client. This includes: cleaning the mind clutter, confronting uncomfortable situations, tackling unfinished tasks, dealing with unwanted "stuff," resolving triggers, and forgiving unfulfilled expectations. All of these are items that might snatch you out of present time. Let's deal with each one.

Readying Yourself to Be Present

Two issues that could stop you from being fully present are rehashing the past or projecting into the future. When you rehash the past, you replay conversations or concerns in your mind. For example, imagine that when your spouse left the house this morning, he or she forgot to say good-bye properly. Rehashing the recent past might sound like this: "Why didn't he say good-bye? Is he mad at me? He is probably worried about the presentation he will be giving this morning. I should have made his breakfast and prepared his coffee just the way he likes it. He wanted to wear his blue shirt, but it's in the wash. He is probably mad at me because I didn't wash and iron his shirt. I didn't have time. I should have picked up the dry cleaning. He has two other blue shirts at the dry cleaners. I should have made time for that . . . if the dog wasn't sick. Oops, I forgot the medicine the vet prescribed for the dog! I hope his presentation goes well. I wanted to wish him good luck . . . if he'd only said good-bye!" This mental conversation is an example of rehashing the past. If the internal conversation engages without your knowledge, you are unaware of your thoughts and they are, in turn, on "automatic pilot."

An example of projecting into the future might sound like this: "I really want tonight's dinner party to go perfectly. If that business deal is going to go forward, things better be perfect. I have to buy salmon. It must be organic because they are very food-conscious, and I checked on their food preferences and requirements. Did I ask them about drinks? Uh-oh, I think I forgot. I don't even know if they drink alcohol. Should I get red or white wine, or just sparkling water? What if they're wine con-noisseurs? What will I serve? How could I have forgotten to ask? Do they eat sugar? Maybe I should go to the bakery and buy some pastries for dessert, but what if they don't eat sugar? Fruit is a better choice. Michael hates bananas; they turn brown if cut in advance. What if I squeeze some lemon juice on them, or is that apples? Berries would be nice. Maybe strawberry shortcake. Then they can choose among berries, whipped cream, or shortbread. What should I wear? Not too casual, but not too dressy, something in-between. Should I bring up the business deal or let it be social? If I bring it up, they might think I am pushy. Better stay away from politics, too, and religion, oh dear . . . what can we talk about?" This mental conversation is an example of projecting into the future and con-sequently being out of present time. An unlimited number of scenarios that you could imagine can take you out of present time. The key is for you to clean your vessel so that you are aware, tuned in, and will notice if and when your mind starts to rehash or projects into the future.

Cleaning the Mind Clutter

When you delay the inevitable, you also clutter the vessel. For instance, if you know you must schedule a teeth cleaning, a mammogram, or a colonoscopy, and you keep putting it off rather than setting an appoint-ment, you attach a mental "clothespin" to part of your consciousness.

Every time you attach these clothespins, you tie up parts of your mind with unnecessary items that you don't want to forget. Clothespins involve all types of tasks like balancing your checkbook, filing your receipts, filling out your expense reports, completing your taxes, paint touch-ups, hanging pictures, getting an oil change, and so on. Having lists of tasks or goals is a positive thing when you write them down and accomplish them. Having mental clothespins robs you of energy, wastes brain cells, and "clutters your brain."

Confronting Uncomfortable Situations

Another way to keep yourself from being fully present is to avoid confronting uncomfortable situations. For instance, if you have a houseguest or a grown child who is planning to move out of your house and the date keeps being postponed, your mental conversation can preoccupy your thoughts. Inside you feel that it is time for you to have your home back, but you don't mention anything to avoid the confrontation and discomfort. Each day you spend time and energy wondering what to do about the situation. This creates more clutter in your head rather than resolving the situation. Having conversations in your head about the situation does not resolve it. You don't want to create an upset, nor do you want the person to be angry with you. At the same time, you want your space back, and each day that passes makes you more disconnected from yourself and your wishes. You hope something will magically resolve the issues without you having to do anything. Regardless of what thoughts you harbor about the unresolved situation, it consumes your energy and depletes part of your life force.

Julie's thirty-two-year-old daughter and ten-year-old granddaughter had been discussing moving out of Julie's home for over a year. Julie had a hard time bringing up the uncomfortable subject. She didn't want to offend anyone, least of all to alienate her daughter and granddaughter. She was so worried about the situation that she scheduled a coaching session. In the session she figured out the right time, place, words, and tone to communicate her wishes to her daughter. When she finally addressed and resolved the issue, a new level of clarity, honesty, and energy were restored to all three.

Tackling Unfinished Tasks

Another situation that clutters your brain is when you say that you are going to accomplish something, like cleaning out the garage, completing the landscaping, or meeting your quota at work. If you never get the task done, it not only clutters your consciousness, it becomes an issue as to whether you can ultimately trust your word. This in turn creates even more distance from yourself. These incomplete tasks or broken promises act like a magnet, attracting more lack of trust and self-doubt. Every time you say you want something but do nothing to make it happen, you create more distance between you and self.

Dealing with Unwanted "Stuff"

Unwanted "stuff" in your home and office also act like clothespins on your consciousness. Each piece of "unchosen stuff" fills your space with the energy labeled *"it doesn't matter." It doesn't matter* that I have the fondue pot my Aunt Sara gave me. It was a sweet gesture, even though I don't eat fondue, and I'll never use it. *It doesn't matter* that I don't clean out that utility drawer. I can't find anything, and lots of the stuff is obsolete, but no one cares. *It doesn't matter* that I have six months of receipts that need to be cataloged. No one knows but me. The point is that *you* know. The most important person, who is in charge of your integrity, knows—*you*! If the situation isn't the way you want it to be, and you put up with it, you create more distance between you and yourself. Whether it is a pile of papers on your desk, a pile of receipts, a pile of books next to your bed, or a pile of clothes to go to charity, they remind you that you are putting up with suboptimal conditions that are not what you want. If you are going to support others in having their lives become the way they want, you don't need to be perfect, but you do need to live up to the standards and expectations that you have established for yourself. If you are saying one thing and doing something else, then you are "out of integrity" with yourself.

Resolving Triggers

Another aspect of cleaning the vessel is eliminating your triggers. A trigger is a restimulation of suppressed feelings from a past incident that caused embarrassment, humiliation, diminishment, or pain. The trigger is similar enough to the initial experience to exhume the suppressed feelings. The trigger may be a tone of voice, a gesture, a word, or an action. For example, Helena, a client, had a rage-filled mother who used to yell at her when she was a child and simultaneously raise her right eyebrow. As an adult, Helena would get triggered every time someone raised his or her eyebrow. As a boy, Tim's dad used to say, "What is the matter with you?" and he always felt diminished. Now when anyone says that phrase to Tim, he feels disproportionately embarrassed and defensive. Louis grew up in a large family in which everyone constantly interrupted each other. When he sits in a staff meeting and everyone talks over him, he shrinks into a small child. These triggers take Helena, Tim, and Louis out of the present moment, and are catalysts for unpleasant and painful feelings from the past. Triggers can also evoke positive memories of nostalgic and sentimental moments from the past. The scent of perfume, the physical resemblance to a favorite relative, the sound of "our song" in the background can all bring back sweet memories that will also take you out of the present moment. The clue that a trigger is occurring is that the response is disproportionate to the stimulus. If there is excessive energy in response to the stimulus, then it is most likely a trigger. When you have become aware of your triggers, owned them, and defused them, they will no longer dictate and control your reactions. Releasing, clearing out, and healing your triggers is another step to cleaning the vessel.

Forgiving Unfulfilled Expectations

Another step to cleaning the vessel is to eliminate anything for which you haven't forgiven yourself and to resolve all "incompletes" from the past that are hanging over your head. This could involve not living up to your expectations; not being where you'd expected you'd be at a point in your life; taking the easy way out; doing something that isn't in alignment with your values, morals, or standards; or being dishonest with yourself or someone else. If you have ever digressed from your standards or expectations, then self-forgiveness is required to heal the rift. Self-forgiveness is erasing an emotional debt. The debt you have with yourself is labeled "letting yourself down." Forgiveness means that you release yourself from the emotional debt of guilt and shame. You officially release yourself from your personal prison. You can do this by writing a letter to yourself or creating absolution in a mirror. However you do this, make sure that you believe the process.

George had some issues with the IRS. He had neglected to pay his taxes for several years, and it hung over his head. When anyone discussed bookkeeping, accounting, or taxes, he immediately became sheepish and found a way to withdraw from the situation. When he heightened his self-awareness, he noticed that his issues with the IRS were keeping him from being connected to himself. He needed to take hold of the situation, address it, and resolve it to complete cleaning the vessel.

Maria always wanted to be a doctor. She went through premed classes, but when she took her MCAT exams, her scores didn't live up to her expectations. As a result, she did not attend medical school, and she always felt incomplete. For her to clean the vessel, she needed to do one of the following: (1) go back and complete medical school, (2) officially release and absolve herself from this expectation, or (3) create an alterative career path that would fulfill her original objectives in substance if not in form.. In other words, she had to resolve this issue for herself once and for all.

This process of "cleaning the vessel" may sound overwhelming, but it is an ongoing process. Just like eliminating the clutter in your home, cleaning out your in-box, and deleting old e-mails are ongoing processes, eliminating the clutter in your consciousness becomes an integral part of your life. Take on the process one step at a time, and do something each day to eliminate "consciousness clutter." Anything that appears to be a clothespin on your consciousness needs to be cleaned out, forgiven, or healed.

WAYS TO HEIGHTEN AWARENESS

When you are fully present, there is a quiet between your ears. You can hear what is happening around you. You can see what is before you. You can feel what is happening in your body, in your emotions, and in the people around you. You can be fully conscious of what is happening inside of you and outside of you as well. You are open to receive the messages from the universe. You trust yourself, the universe, and the messages to provide guidance for the next choice on your path.

In coaching, being 100 percent where you are means being mindful of how you are, with a quiet mind, connected with yourself, connected with the coachee, and focused on the coachee's wishes and outcomes. With the purpose of serving, you are actively holding the energy field, curiously engaged in everything the coachee says, with all of your attention on the coachee, using all of your brain: right and left hemispheres, and the frontal cortex, which is where choices are made.

It is one thing to say, "Be present!" and it is another thing to know the steps to become fully present. Here are a series of steps that you can take to exercise being fully present in your life and in your sessions.

Daily Journal Keeping

The primary purpose of keeping a journal is to check in with yourself, to monitor your inner world, and to get to know your mind and how it works. When you see your innermost thoughts and feelings on paper, it can change your perception of your reality. In other words, you can begin to separate yourself from your thoughts, feelings, ideas, and your condition. You can also see clearly what you want to do to resolve certain items.

The journal is not like the diary from childhood, where you would record facts, events, and conversations. You can avoid the story, the script, and the drama, if you like. The journal is a tool for self-discovery, which can be used as a receptacle for the mind chatter that plays mental Ping-Pong with choices that must be made. It can be used as a tool to listen to yourself. Frequently, we are unaware of the underlying beliefs or decisions that govern our attitudes and behaviors. Listening through the printed word can enable you to unlock patterns that may eclipse the truth. The journal can be a valuable mirror to see yourself in a new light or from a different angle. You can also use the journal as a tool for validation. You can record your "pats on the back" in your journal to highlight accomplishments and achievements.

There is no "right" way to keep your journal; however, there are some tips that can help you get the most out of the journaling experience:

1. Record your thoughts, feelings, and reactions to people, places, and situations. Focus on your internal experience. You can either write with a pen or you can type on your computer. Do whatever is easy and convenient. Don't get stuck in any mode. Eliminate all excuses.

2. Tell *your* truth to the best of your ability. Then dig deeper, and see if there is some even deeper truth. Ask yourself questions like: What is the truth about that? Is there something even deeper? Listen and write whatever answers you receive. Use the journal to get to the bottom of issues that surface. See if you can release the emotion related to an issue or incident.

3. Whenever possible, use your journal in the midst of conflict. When your emotions are the most intense, you can use your journal as a tool to peel back the layers of the onion and delve beneath the surface to assess what is really going on. For instance, anger often masks the tender, vulnerable feelings that lurk in the shadows of our emotional fabric.

4. When you feel "out of sorts," but you don't know why, use the journal to "download" whatever is there. Don't worry about making sense or being responsible; write whatever you feel, think, sense, judge, and so on. Just write what's there.

5. Forget about punctuation, grammar, syntax, and spelling. No one is going to read your journal but you, so let go of the "rules." Make sure that your writing is legible so that you can read it later, but don't edit, rehearse, censor, or withhold.

6. Have your journal be a "safe place" for you. You can tell all your secrets here, and no one will ever know. You can expand upon your fantasies, fears, frolics, or fun. You can tell your visions, plans, hurts, and joys.

7. Use your journal daily. Set aside a special time every day to write in your journal, or carry it with you and use it on and off throughout the day. Even if you have nothing to say, write that you have nothing to say, but don't go a day without writing. Make this commitment to yourself, and do it.

Weekly Report Writing

Weekly reports are a summary extracted from your daily journal. If you keep your journal faithfully, writing your weekly report will become very easy. In one double-spaced page, you can capture the essence of your week: the highlights, the lessons, what actions are to be taken, illumination of discoveries, and messages. You can keep your weekly reports in a folder on your computer so you can easily track your progress. This is a great way to self-monitor.

Sharing

Every time you share your experience, you externalize your internal reality. Externalizing is helpful because good news becomes reinforced, and others are invited to share in your acknowledgment. When the information you share is less-than-positive, you deplete its power by externalizing it. When you hold on to some secret for fear that others may think ill of you, you give the secret more power. When you share it, you reclaim the power you had given away. This doesn't mean that you must become an extrovert. It is, however, an invitation to practice becoming fully present, being your authentic self, connecting with others, telling your truth, and claiming your time and space.

Processing Issues

When you discover that you are blocked emotionally, mentally, interpersonally, or physically, take note of it so that you can address it. Processing the blocked areas enables you to get unstuck. There are four components to unblocking energy: energy release, healing, forgiveness, and love. In order to heal wounds from the past, all four elements need to be present. In this way, old hurts can be permanently healed. This is another important part to self-development that accompanies the integrity of the coaching process.

Meditating

Meditation can always help you become present. Meditation is a helpful way to practice mindfulness and quieting the mind. Learn it, practice it, and do it often. If you don't know how to meditate, you can go online and search for "meditation training" and receive a plethora of options. There are also books, tapes, and classes available.

Committing to Personal Development

If you determine that your continual growth is an important priority, then you will continue to be involved in your own personal development. This may mean having coaching sessions when you feel the need. The commitment to growth will enable you to determine the most appropriate vehicle for your current situation. Growth can happen on any plane: physical, emotional, metaphysical, psychological, spiritual, financial, organizational, and interpersonal. If you are going to help others, you need to be a living example of the process. Having your personal team of supporters will enable you to stay on track, listen to your messages, and live the process.

Noticing Resistance

When you notice any resistance within you, it helps illuminate reactions that may be coming from the past. Resistance can provide clues to unconscious parts of you that have been hidden from yourself. For instance, you may have resistance to personal development assignments that might lead back to authority issues from childhood. You might invite the resistance, by allowing it to bubble up to the surface, and giving yourself permission to act it out. When you stop resisting your triggers, they will stop running you. The unresolved incidents from the past keep you from being fully present and embracing your future.

Noticing How You Are

Pay attention to your general condition as often as you can each day. This doesn't mean that you become preoccupied with yourself, but rather that you stay tuned in to your general condition. When you notice how you are, you eliminate the possibility of being unconscious.

REQUIRED CORE COMPETENCY CHECKLIST FOR "BRILLIANT" COACHING

Coaching has a lot to do with awareness, since that is an essential element in the process; however, it isn't everything. When you have developed your relationship with self and heightened your awareness, you will be in a position to acquire the additional required skills to become a "brilliant" coach.

A "brilliant" coaching session occurs when you are fully present and in the flow, being your true authentic self. A "brilliant" session dances with energy, combines heart and power, empowers through empathy, and supports the choice that the coachee wants to make. When a "brilliant" session occurs, there is a beautiful exchange of power between two people. The coach, while maintaining control, is in service to the coachee and empowers him or her to make choices. A "brilliant" session means that the coachee had his or her expectations exceeded. It means effortless energy illuminated the objective and provided resolution. It means that the mission was accomplished in an elegant and deeply connected manner.

We use the following list of criteria to provide feedback to our coaches. These criteria measure whether you have adequately mastered the specific behaviors required to become a "brilliant" coach. A "brilliant" coaching session is one in which:

The coach connected with the coachee. Connection is the moment when your energies become merged. When two people are connected, distance, barriers, and withheld communication dissolve. If you are not connected, a coaching session cannot happen. It might be a conversation, but not a session. Connection is the first and most important step in the process. Connection is more than establishing rapport by discussing the weather, traffic, or if there was difficulty finding the location. Connection is energetic. It happens when you have a clean vessel, are open and available, and reach out with your energy field. Ed was concerned about working with the president of a software organization. He usually coached at the middle-management level. Instead of clearing himself on this new challenge, he neglected to connect with his client. The session, although transitional, was not transformational.

The coach clarified time and outcome expectations. Clarification is an essential yet simple matter of addressing the amount of time you will have together and the coachee's expectations. If these expectations are not addressed, it could give rise to uncertainty and/or mind chatter. Establishing your expectations up front eliminates confusion or guessing.

The coach established a clear and achievable objective. Establishing an objective that is clear and doable means that both you and the coachee agree on the focus or topic for your time together. It also means that the objective is realistic to tackle in the time allocated. You want to make sure that the expectations are winnable for both of you.

The coach understood the coachee's objective. Understanding the objective means that you don't proceed until you really "get" what the coachee is saying, and you believe that it is achievable. You may need to clarify, hone, or redefine the objective so that it is the right objective for the time allocated. It also presumes that you empathize with the coachee's experience.

The coach focused attention on coachee. Focusing your attention on the coachee means that you have the ability to shift the locus of your attention onto another. When you are present and focused, you can dedicate your full attention to the coachee for the time you are together.

The coach actively listened. Active listening is more than hearing. When you listen, you concentrate and pay attention to what you hear. When you actively listen, you are sincerely curious and, as such, are engaged in the conversation energetically.

The coach was in flow. When you are in flow, the energy moves easily without constraint. Flow is the steady, unbroken, and continuous stream of energy between two or more people. It is also the psychological and physical experience that results in heightened states of awareness, confidence, and performance. Flow is about alignment and connection with the universal source of energy. Flow is without effort, struggle, or force. When you're in flow, you are in present time as your authentic self, tuned in to what is happening at the moment, allowing the "messages" to come to you.

The coach did what was necessary to stay in flow. This means that if and when you become disconnected, misunderstand something, or get lost or off track, you acknowledge it to yourself and the coachee. In order to stay in flow or to get back in flow, you must tell the truth, honor your feelings, listen to and follow your message, have your actions and your words line up, and operate with integrity. If and when you lose the flow of the session, it can be embarrassing, especially if you are a perfection-ist. It means that you tell the uncomfortable truth that your conscious-ness wandered for a moment. The behaviors that block "flow" are: thinking about what to say, fixating on a word or phrase, "efforting" at figuring out what to say or do, judging what the coachee said, becoming disinterested in the subject of the session, thinking about other people, places, or things, fearing that the content of the session is beyond your capabilities, and trying to do the session perfectly rather than being authentic.

The coach took care of himself or herself. This includes addressing physical things that don't work for you as well as interpersonal issues. You may need to rearrange the chair placement, or you may need to address timeliness if the coachee is late. The coach cannot be more concerned about being liked than about serving the coachee. When the approval syndrome takes over, the desire to be accepted is more important than being authentic and telling the truth. Those are times when you forget to take care of you.

The coach was nonjudgmental. Being nonjudgmental is the corner-stone of the MMS coaching method and is essential to the success of the session. When judgments enter a session, they eliminate the possibility for transformation. Judgments are the cancer of interpersonal dynamics. The coach must suspend judgment of the coachee throughout the session in order for total empowerment to happen.

The coach used heart and power chakras. The chakras are the centers of spiritual power in the body. They are lined up along the spine from the top of the head to the base of the trunk. Knowledge and the conscious ability to adjust your chakras are part of every coaching session. The awareness and practice using a blend of heart energy for unconditional acceptance coupled with power energy that transmits belief in the coachee's infinite abilities will create the ideal androgynous blend. Knowledge of the chakras is the first step to owning your power. Practice is required to achieve mastery over them. (See Chapter 6 for a full explanation of chakras.)

The coach adjusted second and sixth chakras. The reason we ask for this is to eliminate any confusion in the subtle interpersonal dynamics of a session. The second chakra is associated with sexuality and is inappropriate in a coaching session. The sixth chakra is the third eye or "knowing" and as such belongs in a psychic session, but not in a coaching session because the coach needs to embrace his or her "not knowing" for the coachee. You will still be using your intuition, but it will come in the form of curious questions rather than in the form of knowing answers. Experiencing a gut feeling or "message" is much different from knowing what is going on for another person.

The coach asked about related feelings. In each session, at each significant moment, feelings need to be addressed. Feelings are so integral to the process of coaching that they must be considered and explored. If the coachee is to make an integrated choice, then both the thoughts and feelings about each separate issue must be pursued. Feelings are the lights on the dashboard of life.

The coach restated information without parroting. Restatement is when the coach states what he or she has heard to anchor the shared understanding of the situation. Restatement comes after a chunk of information has been revealed in order to ensure accuracy and agreement before proceeding.

The coach recapped at strategic moments. Recapping is a tool that is used to summarize what has transpired at four points in a session: (1) when you have reached an information saturation point, (2) when you have reached an impasse, (3) when you have come to a crossroads in the session, or (4) when there is a need for clarification, alignment, direction, or a reality check. Recapping enables the coachee to track progress, clarifies inaccuracies and misunderstandings, helps the coachee clarify direction, ensures both people are aligned, reduces misunderstandings, eliminates ambiguities, deepens the connection, and affirms the coachee's reality. Recapping enables the coachee to provide direction. Recapping must happen at least once in every session.

The coach acknowledged when confused or stuck. Acknowledgment enables you to reestablish your authenticity. It allows you to get back on track with the session and prevents you from pretending or covering up the disconnection. When you acknowledge the confusion or "stuckness," it helps to reconnect the coach with the coachee. Transformational coaching only happens when you are being truly authentic.

The coach asked clear, open-ended questions. Asking open-ended questions creates an atmosphere in which the coachee can choose. Asking closed-ended questions steers the coachee in a direction. Open-ended questions enable the coachee to examine his or her motivation and behavior and make clear choices.

The coach used "clues" to generate questions. Using clues keeps the flow of the session moving forward. Clues emanate naturally from the coachee's answers and lead organically to the likely next question. When you use the clues, you don't have to think up "smart" questions to ask, but rather take your cues directly from the coachee.

The coach maintained objectivity. If you maintain objectivity, you don't become so involved in the coachee's concerns that you lose your perspective. Objectivity is essential if you are to support another. Being objective means that you don't climb inside the issue with the coachee but rather remain at arms' length with the issue while staying connected to the person. This may sound like a paradox, and it is. A paradox is where seemingly opposite items are both simultaneously true.

The coach used coachee's choice of words. You listen closely to the coachee's word choice and do not paraphrase or superimpose your own ideas on the coachee's situation. When you use the coachee's words, there is an experience of validation and a demonstration that you recreate the coachee's reality. When you change the coachee's words, an experience of feeling discounted, discredited, and diminished can result. When you use the coachee's words, he or she feels the antithesis: heard, validated, and honored.

The coach demonstrated sincere interest. When you demonstrate sincere interest, you show with your eyes, your body language, and your focus that you are keenly interested in what is being said. You also show your genuine concern through establishing a rhythm of asking open-ended questions. When you find your rhythm, you get into the flow of the session.

The coach asked about vision or ideal outcome. In every session there is an appropriate moment to ask about the desired outcome or fantasy. There are numerous ways to ask this: How would you like this story to end? If you had a magic wand, and you waved it in this situation, what would the outcome be? Ideally, how would you like things to work out? What is your vision of how things could ideally be? There isn't one right question, but there is an appropriate moment to ask this question. Each session is uniquely different; however, in each session the coach will ask a question regarding the coachee's preferred image of positive resolution.

The coach believed in the coachee's ability. If the coach doubts the coachee's ability, it will be transmitted through words, gestures, tone of voice, expression, or through the energy field. If the coach doesn't believe that the coachee can have what he or she truly wants, then the session needs to end. The coach must not take the coachee's time, energy, and money if he or she doesn't believe in the coachee. This is an internal ethical question that the coach must ask himself or herself.

The coach chauffeured the session effortlessly. Chauffeuring means that the coach is in the driver's seat but takes the session where the coachee wants to go. It is not acceptable for the coach to "drive" the session where the coach thinks the coachee needs to go (for his or her own good). If this happens, it means that the coach has opened his or her third eye, knows better than the coachee what is best for him or her, and has decided to take control and do whatever the coach wants. Chauffeuring is egoless and grounded yet anchored in "not knowing" what is best for the coachee.

The coach acknowledged mirrors when helpful. In every coaching session there is a mirror. The mirror is the reflection of something for the coach to learn. The mirror could be an acknowledgment of progress for the coach, or it could be the discovery of a blocked area. There is always a mirror in every session, whether it is in the actual form of the session or in the challenges the coachee is encountering. Looking at the mirrors always provides the coach with a gift. The gift may be readily apparent, or it may be concealed; however, if you look a little deeper you will always discover it. The gift is in the form of a mirror. The person sitting across from you is not there by accident. There is something about the issue, situation, or emotion the coachee is experiencing that mirrors back some aspect of your life, either in the past or the present. The mirror can be an acknowledgment, a trigger, an illumination, or a wake-up call. If the issue is something that you have already addressed and broken through, it will be an acknowledgment. If the situation is something that reminds you of a similar situation you are grappling with, it is an illumination. If the emotion shows you an aspect of yourself that is stuck, the session is a wake-up call. You will always see something about yourself in every session that you experience. When you complete your session, ask yourself the question, "What is the mirror in this session?" When you ask that question, and you look closely, you will receive a gift regarding your own personal evolution.

The coach supported rather than directed. Supporting means coming from underneath without ego attachment. Directing means coming from above with the agenda of looking good, doing it well, or being "right." The fear of looking stupid, being wrong, asking dumb questions, and not knowing the answers will often nudge a coach in training into directing the session. It is only when you relinquish your attachment to your ego needs that you can truly serve the coachee. To achieve this "clean" place, you must trust yourself and the process in the void. When there is nothing to hold on to, you must trust that the coachee truly does know what he or she wants.

The coach utilized empathetic unattachment. "Empathetic unattachment" is the paradoxical energy that enables you to stay connected to the coachee without becoming emotionally enmeshed in their issue. Subjectivity is not helpful; neither is disconnection. It is the paradoxical blend of empathy with unattachment that creates this delicate balance. This is similar to "maintained objectivity," but empathetic unattachment focuses more on the open-heart, emotional connection, rather than the mental focus.

The coach brought the session to closure. In each session, there is a beginning, a middle, and an end. For a session to be complete, it must be brought to a close. There must be a natural and organic closure to the session that is chauffeured effortlessly by the coach.

The coachee made a choice. The purpose of each session is for the coachee to make a choice. Choice is to select freely that which you want from a series of alternatives. In the coaching session, the coach helps the coachee sort out the options, examine thoughts and feelings, determine the ideal outcome, and select his or her preference after assessing all of the alternatives. If no choice is made, then the session has not been "brilliant."

The coachee left with a plan. The coachee needs to have his or her own set of action steps to move the progress of the session forward. This is often called homework or the action steps to be implemented. It is important for the coachee to demonstrate commitment to the session and the progress that is being made. The coachee must take the discoveries from the session and apply them in tangible ways.

The coachee knew post-session support options. Before the coachee exits the coaching environment, it is important for him or her to know what is expected. For instance, is it okay to e-mail the coach? Is it okay to call the coach? If calling is agreeable, what number should be used? In other words, what type of communication is expected and appreciated between sessions, and how much is anticipated? This should be articulated and agreed upon before the coachee departs so that there is clarity.

The session felt complete. Complete means there was nothing left to say. Everything that pertained to the subject was covered or presented. In revisiting the original objective, the cycle is completed. With the final restatement, closure is brought to the session, and it is acknowledged by the coachee that it is complete.

The coach was unattached to the outcome. When the coach becomes more invested than the coachee, the session becomes codependent, and the balance becomes skewed. The coachee must always be more invested in his or her situation and outcome than the coach for the proper energy balance to be in place.

The "wow factor" was present. During every "brilliant" session there is an unexpected moment in which the coachee discovers something about himself or herself and the situation. It is an "aha moment," an epiphany, or an illumination that shifts the energy from the coachee being "at the effect" of the situation to becoming "at cause" in their circumstances. The "wow factor" doesn't happen in every session, but it is always present in a "brilliant" session. Another way you can detect the "wow factor" is in the illumination of the coachee's face. An inner light will appear when the discovery has been revealed.

Those are all of the specific behaviors that we look for when we give feedback to our coaching students. When all of those behaviors are demonstrated, the session qualifies as "brilliant." When you have experienced a "brilliant" session, you know how it feels to be without agenda or ego and to serve your client from a pure place.

The "brilliant" aspect moves the coaching process from transitional to transformational. It happens when the coachee feels empowered to transform his or her life from what is to what could be. This happens in a safe environment where it is possible to consider unlimited possibilities. It emerges organically through a connection that is unattached to any specific outcome. It feels like the ring of truth at a very deep level.

Coaching is a precious process that gently and powerfully helps another make a choice. Choices involve change, and change can only happen when awareness is present. The transformational quality happens through the conscious interpersonal weaving of two people's energies. Choices happen when a safe and aware environment encourages the truth to be spoken, and the coach is ready to listen and empower without judgment.

Listening and Connecting

"The important thing is not to stop questioning.
Curiosity has its own reason for existing."
Albert Einstein

*L*istening is not the same as hearing. Hearing and listening are different aspects of a similar function. Hearing is the perception of sound, while listening requires that you pay attention to something that is communicated in order to take it into account. Hearing is passive, and listening can be either passive or active. You can overhear someone's conversation, or you can pay attention to the person who is talking to you.

Listening is extremely important in coaching. If you don't know how to actively listen, you will surely miss some critical pieces of information that will affect your ability to respond and support another. Listening is a learned skill, and there are many things that can block your capacity to listen. In order to be a "brilliant" coach, you want to master the art of listening. Most of all, you want to be able to listen to the silence without having to fill it with words, sounds, or noise. In the musical *The Fantasticks,* there is a line that says, "Listen with the insides of your hands to the silent sounds of silence." If we are interested and curious, then listening is a natural state. Let's examine what gets in the way of listening.

THINGS THAT PREVENT LISTENING

In the stimulus-filled world in which we live, there is a plethora of distractions to challenge your ability to actively listening to what is being communicated. Here are several of them.

Preoccupation

Being preoccupied means that something is redirecting your consciousness. Imagine that you were just diagnosed with cancer, or your spouse said he or she wanted a divorce, or your boss told you that you were being laid off. It is completely understandable in all of these situations to be preoccupied with the information you just received. All three scenarios have the potential of drastically altering your life. If you hadn't seen them coming, you would be alarmed. The words would give your mind a complete preoccupation and the potential of spinning out of control in many different directions.

Even in less dire circumstances, people become preoccupied with matters that take them away from the person who is sitting directly across from them. For instance, you could be preoccupied with what you are going to wear to an important event, with the pain in your lower back, with the preparations for an upcoming meeting, with concerns about a loved one who is ill, or with just about anything that takes hold of your consciousness and won't let go. Sometimes these preoccupations are understandable because of the nature of the information, and at other times it may appear as if you are obsessing about something insignificant. In either case, awareness will help you determine whether the preoccupation is understandable or obsessive. When you become aware of the mind chatter, you can then determine what you want to do with the conversation in your head Here are some options to consider:

Do you want to write it down?

Do you want to talk it out?

Do you need to obtain clarification or additional information to quiet the voices?

As a coach, you need to be able to silence the voices in your mind at will so you can pay full attention and listen to everything that is being said ... and to what is *not* being said. The steps to quieting the voices are to (1) become aware of the preoccupation or mind chatter, (2) determine what you want to do about it, (3) choose an action to quiet the voices in your head, and (4) focus 100 percent attention on your client.

Rehearsing Lines or Responses

When you are preparing your response to what was previously said, you cannot listen to what is currently being said. With one voice talking to you from inside your mind and another voice talking to you from outside your head, your attention becomes split. If you are aware, you always have a choice. If you have been trained in debating or in the skill of argumentation, then you may already be focused on the voice in your head, automatically preparing your rebuttal. If you are listening to the voice in your head telling you what to say next, then you cannot completely listen to the person speaking to you. In order to listen, you need to be fully present. To be present in a dialogue, you need to let go of having the right answer, delivering the intelligent or witty comeback, having the last word, or ultimately being right. You need to do something unimpressive, uninspiring, and uncomplicated ... which is to just listen. It may sound way too simple, but it requires a fair amount of decluttering in order to be a really good listener.

Absorbing Information

Some conversations are filled with detailed content. If you are unfamiliar with the subject matter, or if there is a great deal of information, you may constantly repeat the words in your mind in an effort to try to remember what you are hearing. If you don't have a pad and pen available, the pressure to remember becomes intensified. Likewise, when someone speaks with a heavy accent, you may struggle to understand the words.

Stephen was doing a session with Lillian regarding her relationship with her father. Lillian, an Italian, was talking so rapidly that Stephen had a hard time keeping up with her. When Lillian said the word *pedestal*, Stephen missed the word. The word was a key component to the session, however. Had he not gone back to pick it up, the session would have been extremely difficult to track. The word *pedestal* was symbolic of the relationship that needed to be shifted for Lillian to be empowered as an adult.

There may be times when you want to repeat what the coachee says to see if you can understand what he or she is saying in the context of the sentence. Trying to absorb, understand, or avoid forgetting information are all activities that will impact your ability to listen accurately. If you are aware that this is going on, use a pen and paper to capture the information while letting your client know that you want to accurately document what is being said.

Blocking/Closing to New Information

There are times when you hear something that is disconcerting or shocking. When you hear something you didn't anticipate, your mind might engage in asking you how you are going to deal with this information. Since the coaching process is confidential, intimate, and honest, there can easily be surprises in contrast to the client's public persona. It could be a financial matter regarding a debt to another, a secret affair, or a revelation of someone's private unhappiness.

Laura was coaching Margaret about her inability to speak up for herself. At a certain moment, Margaret mentioned that she had been abused in her childhood. It took Laura a few minutes to recover because of the outrage she felt regarding Margaret's situation. When she grounded herself, Laura took some deep breaths and allowed Margaret to formulate her strategy on how she was going to heal the past and start standing up for herself verbally.

If you were coaching a celebrity who acknowledged that he was on drugs, that she was bulimic, or that he had a sex addiction, you might be taken aback. In situations like these, you must get yourself to snap back into the here and now with the facts as they are being presented at the time.

Another situation in which you might block the information is when a client presents you with information that you feel is way over your head. Perhaps you are having a coaching session with a physicist whose technical expertise is light-years beyond yours. You might be intimidated, and you might just tune out.

You might also find that you have a mental block to a specific subject. Imagine that you have a block to numbers. Your client asks, "I want to review our financial projections for next year with you. I brought the profit and loss statement from this year along with our balance sheet." If you decided that you couldn't read a profit and loss statement or a balance sheet, then you might react in a negative manner that might block your client's request. You could end up having a conversation with yourself that sounds like this: "What am I going to do? He will discover that I'm unqualified and inept in this area. What can I say?" Ultimately, being authentic is your best policy. When you tell the truth, it gets you back on track and relieves you from having to pretend to be something you are not. Opening up to all possibilities will help you grow as a coach.

Distractions

In a perfect world, with no distractions, it is easier to listen. When something distracts you, it becomes more challenging to pay attention. A recurring noise, a flickering light, people speaking outside the room, sirens or horns honking outside the building all will attempt to distract you from your focus. The world is full of distractions trying to steal your attention. It is up to you to minimize the distractions you can control. Acknowledge the ones you cannot control so they don't dominate you, and then refocus. You need to take care of yourself so that whatever noise or light distracts you doesn't become an obsession. If you suppress them, they have more power over you. If you address them and acknowledge what you experience, you take back the power. The manner in which you handle the distractions says a lot about you.

Lack of Interest

When the subject matter is not engaging or if you don't have any interest in the content, it will take more of you than you ever imagined to find something to be curious about. If the focus of a coaching session is on how to market a paving company, how to sell more hamburgers, or how to control a growing population of rodents, you might need to dig deep to find your innate curiosity. If the subject really doesn't interest you, and you could care less about the outcome, you must find some aspect of the conversation that could possibly engage you. If you can't become intrigued in the subject matter, then perhaps you could become inspired by the passion of the person taking on the task, or maybe there is something you could learn from the coachee's approach that would add to your knowledge. Find some kernel to which you can attach your consciousness and focus on that. Acknowledge to yourself that you are making a deliberate effort to find a point of connection. If none of these proposed options is possible, you probably want to refer the client to another coach.

Preconceived Notions

When you enter a coaching session with preconceived ideas about a person, a situation, or a subject, it makes it more difficult to pay attention and to be genuinely fascinated because you already think you know everything that is about to be said. You may be having a session with a close friend who is moving to a new apartment, and since you know her so well you believe that you already know all of her issues and concerns. You have to set aside your knowledge or "knowingness" about the situation and approach it with what they call in Zen, "beginner's mind," which allows you to find your inquisitiveness. This enables you to become interested and let go of knowing what is best for her.

Getting Stuck on a Word or Idea

There are moments when people use a term, a phrase, or a reference that stops you dead in your tracks. You pause and start to think, "What was that word? I don't know what that means." In a session with a Swiss computer programmer who was focused on marketing, I found myself in that position. At one moment he said, completely out of the blue, "Oh, it's all just cows!" I looked at him quizzically and thought to myself, "Why is he talking about cows? I don't remember any discussion about animals. Did I miss a whole chunk of the conversation? How do I respond to that statement? I have no idea what he is talking about!" I finally found the right moment to ask him what he was referring to. He said, "Cows, you know?" I said naively, "I am sorry. I just don't get the connection between computers, marketing, and cows. Can you help me understand the connection?" He raised his voice and articulated clearly, "C-H-A-O-S, *cows* is what I said." I replied, "In my country, we call that *chaos* (kay-oss)." We both had a good laugh, and I learned something about listening that day that I will never forget. If I hadn't spoken up, I would have been fixated on his word "cows," not hearing any of the subsequent paragraphs that came after. When you become stuck on a word, phrase, or an idea, address it, and get reconnected to the client and the client's objective, and do it as soon as you know that you are fixated.

Language Barriers

I have taught, given speeches, and been interviewed in over thirty countries around the world. I know from firsthand experience that it is easy to have language challenges affect your ability to listen and understand what another person says. I was having a conversation with one of our licensees in Holland. We were discussing a large electronics company when he said, "I think they had great turnover last year." In my definition, *turnover* is far from good or great; it means that people are leaving the company. I asked him how turnover could be good. He looked at me with disbelief and said, "What do you mean?" I said, "How can people leaving the company be a good thing?" He said, "Turnover is the amount of business transacted in a certain period resulting in gross revenues." I was amazed that our understanding of the same word in the same language had such dramatically different meaning. Later, I looked up the word and saw that both of us were right. In Europe they generally use one of the definitions given, while in the United States we use another. If I hadn't asked, or if I had only had the conversation with myself instead of including him, the outcome would have been much different. I learned something because I was willing to ask what seemed to me to be a stupid question.

Time

When you are concerned about time, it is difficult to listen to what is being said. Roberta's client was extremely late on account of an accident blocking the freeway. This was her last appointment of the day, and she was leaving directly from the office to catch a plane. As the minutes ticked by, she found herself becoming more and more anxious. Finally, her client arrived, but in the middle of the session she found herself unable to focus on what he was saying. Her thoughts were on traffic, crowds, getting through security, and trying to make her flight. She was so distracted that she had to address it and say to him, "I think we need to reschedule. Otherwise I could miss my flight, and I do want to give you my undivided attention." Take the risk and speak up rather than internalizing the nervousness and worry.

Jumping to Conclusions

There are times when everyone tends to jump to conclusions. You hear the beginning of the story and associate it with something in your own life, and the assumptions engage. When Jan shared with Tony that she had been raised by an alcoholic parent, Tony responded, "So was I! I know just what you went through. I've been there." What Tony didn't know was that Jan's situation was much more extreme than his, and consequently, her scars were much deeper. The sharing might have connected the two people, but as a result of the assumptions, more distance was created. When you stay with your curious listening rather than jumping to conclusions, it reinforces your respect for the other person and keeps the session pure without projection.

THE FIVE LEVELS OF COMMUNICATION

To be an effective communicator, you need to be aware of the five levels of communication. If you are listening closely, you will be able to discern the level of communication in the conversation. The five levels are:

1. **Clichéd conversation.** The first level of communication doesn't require any investment or involvement from you. It is the most superficial level and consists of a greeting, a salutation, or a clichéd comment that doesn't require any interaction.
2. **Reporting the facts.** Examples of the second level of communication are the newspaper, TV news and weather, or a report describing some happening, such as a sale or an upcoming event.
3. **Judgments.** At the third level of communication, you expose a part of yourself. This level involves judgments, which requires taking a stand on something.

4. **Feelings.** All feelings require you to expose part of your internal world. Feelings are more vulnerable than judgments, and at the fourth level you reveal your emotional connection to the subject matter.

5. **Peak communication.** This is the fifth and the most connected level. Peak communication happens between soul mates, twins, those with past-life connections, some siblings, some parents and children, some spouses, dharmic lovers, and other people who are deeply in love. Peak communication means that you are so connected that you rarely need words. You can complete each other's sentences, and when one of you thinks something, the other says it.

Since setting the expectation of peak communication in every coaching session would be unrealistic, we set the fourth level as the goal. You may have sessions that reach the fifth level, but you will address feelings in every coaching session that you do.

THE DIFFERENCE BETWEEN FEEDBACK AND CRITICISM

It is not always what you say but rather the manner in which you say it that makes the difference. There is a fine line between feedback and criticism, and you need to be especially careful that you don't cross that line. Feedback is the variety of comments regarding your attitude, behavior, mannerisms, techniques, and communication level that is presented in a manner that is useful, empowering, and easily deployable for future behavior change, choices, and further development. When you receive feedback you need to breathe, stay open, be willing to learn, let go of any defensiveness, empower the person to give you feedback, and restate what you have learned so you can both agree that you are on the same page, perceiving the situation in the same manner.

Criticism consists of comments toward you that are judgmental in tone, point out your faults, or attack something about you that cannot be changed. Criticism is rarely helpful, more often hurtful, and frequently will make you feel bad, wrong, or cause you to become defensive.

While conducting the MMS Coach Training, it is always our intention to provide feedback that is helpful to develop coaching skills. It is never our intention to hurt our trainees or make them feel anything less than esteemed. You don't necessarily need to be verbal to communicate criticism.

NONVERBAL AND OTHER INDIRECT COMMUNICATION

People communicate with their bodies what is on their minds. When someone taps a foot incessantly, it makes it difficult to pay attention to what that person is saying. When a client sighs every few minutes, it can start you counting the sighs rather than listening to the words. When someone sits with arms and legs closed in a warm room, it is time to pay attention and address what the physical body is saying that may be different from the client's words. It is very important to address body language that sends a message that is different from what is being said verbally. If your client says he or she is angry but is smiling, mention it. If the nervous tapping continues, address it rather than trying to ignore it. Sometimes the nonverbal communication is trying to get your attention, especially when the person has difficulty articulating what is really going on that he or she may not be in touch with.

The coach sends nonverbal cues as well. You must pay attention to your posture. Sitting too far back and crossing arms or legs could not only block energy, but it could send a signal to the client that there is a break in the communication.

Behaviors That Show the Listener Is Not Interested

Body Language, Interrupting, and other challenges

Lack of eye contact/body language. If your client won't look at you, it could mean one of five possibilities: (1) there is a cultural difference present, and eye contact is considered rude in the coachee's culture, (2) the coachee is embarrassed about something, (3) the coachee is trying to hide something, (4) the coachee's thoughts are elsewhere, and he or she is not listening to what you are saying, or (5) the coachee could be attracted to you.

Interrupting. If your client keeps interrupting you, it is a signal that you have lost the flow. You probably need to be still and listen to what the coachee has to say. When there is an opening, you can ask the next appropriate question. Interrupting is a sign that your client is not listening to you.

Rambling. If either your client or you start to ramble, it means that someone isn't listening, and the flow has stopped. It is difficult to interrupt for fear of being rude. The ability to break into a steady stream of words in a nonoffensive manner is developed with practice. If you find yourself waiting for the right moment to intervene, consider making physical contact and saying, "Sorry to interrupt you, but I have a question." This could also be an opportunity for restatement or a review of the objective. If you are paying attention, you will pick up the clue as to when to interrupt. If you hear yourself rambling on and on, stop, take a breath, and refocus on the objective and your coachee.

Sentence completing/word filling. If your client is completing your sentences, he or she is anticipating what you might share. In jumping ahead, the coachee is thinking he or she knows what you are about to say. There are two possibilities: the coachee could be right or the coachee could be wrong. If the coachee's completion of your sentence is not correct, be gentle when you provide the correct version of how the sentence should end. It can be embarrassing to the coachee to discover that his or her ending is not the right one or that the connection is not as aligned as the coachee had imagined. If this happens, acknowledge it, at least to yourself, and then get back on track.

Behaviors That Show the Listener Is Interested

Conscious Communication Cues

Eye contact. If you and your client are both from a culture that values eye contact, then show your interest by gently looking into one of your coachee's eyes. Show your interest and let the coachee feel affirmed and important with your eye connection. If the coachee is from a culture that considers eye contact rude, then be conscious of looking away every so often, so you don't make the other person uncomfortable. You don't want your eye connection to turn into a stare. Staring and glaring can appear confrontational and make the coachee ill at ease.

Body language. Face your client with your body, and make sure there are no tables in the way. Make sure that your arms and legs aren't crossed, and keep your arms and legs from tapping, bouncing, or swinging. Do your best to sit straight without looking awkward. You want to present a quiet body and a quiet mind. You also want to sit so that the energy can flow through you to the coachee easily without constriction.

Restatement. Restatement and recapping are two of the best ways to discipline your listening skills. Knowing that you will need to feed back what you have heard is one of the best ways to ensure that you are seriously paying attention to what is being said. In aviation, pilots are required to restate what they have heard from air traffic control. The conversations are redundant; however, there is little room for misunderstandings. You don't need to become a pilot to effectively use restatement; just know that when you are uncertain, it is best to check out the accuracy of the transmission and reception of the message.

Self-disclosure. When you detect a similarity, a concern, a fear, or a special interest in a session, acknowledge it rather than keeping it to yourself. In every session there is a gift for the coach. The "mirror" shows you either how far you've come or where you need to focus more attention or effort in your own life. Alice was coaching Simone when she saw her own housing challenge sitting across from her. Alice had been unsuccessfully looking for a new home for two years. When Simone talked about whether she should decorate her present home or move to a new location, Alice saw her own issue undeniably. If Alice hadn't acknowledged her own housing challenge, she would never have been able to stay with Simone in the present moment. Although she conducted a good session, Alice saw that she needed to take action on her own needs so that she could model the behavior she was encouraging in Simone. If she hadn't taken action, her clients might mirror her "stuck" aspects and, consequently, produce limited results. Alice immediately scheduled a session with her coach to see what was going on. With the clarity and acceleration from the session, Alice gave notice, manifested her dream apartment, and moved within thirty days.

Sounds/words that confirm. Words like *um, ah, oh, okay, good,* and *yeah* all communicate to your client that you are engaged and paying attention. Use them from time to time, especially when your client has a long story to share. Be careful not to overuse them. In addition, you can interject leading words such as *because . . . , and . . . , so . . . , then . . .* instead of complete sentences to encourage your client to continue and get to the heart of the matter. You needn't ask complete questions if the interaction doesn't warrant it. Consider also the simple and concise three-word prompts. They are: Where are you? What is happening? Talk out loud. Tell me more. These pithy laserlike probes will keep the flow going and keep the attention off of you.

Reaching out empathetically. Empathy is essential in every session. You want to be careful that you don't slide unconsciously into sympathy. The blend that we are searching for is called "empathetic unattachment." Empathy extends your feelings to recreate what your client is feeling. The unattachment maintains your objectivity so that you don't become enmeshed with your client in the issue. Most people either move toward sympathy or they disconnect. Empathetic unattachment produces extraordinary results because your heart is open while you simultaneously empower the client to resolve his or her own challenge.

Asking single questions. When you ask two or three questions in succession without allowing the client to respond to each one individually, you overload and confuse the client and break the flow, sending the message that you are not listening. Ask only *one* question at a time. Then pause, listen, stay connected, and send energy to the coachee. Remember, you don't want to clutter the space, but rather clarify, simplify, and frame.

JUDGMENTS

The definition of judgment is to form an opinion of someone, to criticize or condemn another. Judgments are the cancer of interpersonal relationships.

Negative judgments originate from insecurity, insufficiency, and inadequacy. They are a way of feeling superior to the person you are judging. They diminish someone else in order for you to feel better about yourself. Judgments protect you from feeling vulnerable and exposed. They act like a protective shell, keeping people out and buffering you from feeling less than others. When you find yourself judging someone, ask yourself, "What is the feeling underneath the judgment?" Usually the feeling is one that you don't want to feel. The feeling is inadequate, insufficient, unable, or not good enough. In order to avoid the feeling about yourself, you unconsciously formulate a judgment about the other person. The feeling that you don't want to feel turns into a judgment and becomes projected onto the other person. When you start to feel a judgment, ask yourself what you are feeling. If you can connect with your actual feeling, it will diffuse the judgment. In this light, every judgment becomes a "gift" because it gives you back a disowned piece of yourself. Judgments say more about you than they do about the person you are judging.

If you are judging your client, ask yourself three things: (1) What am I feeling? (2) What might this situation be mirroring back to me? and (3) Is this judgment serving me or getting in my way? When you receive an answer, write it down. Then ask yourself what you want to do about it. Schedule your action step, and then get it done. Acknowledge yourself for the results you have seen that are mirrored back to you in a positive manner.

SUSPENDING JUDGMENT

Suspending judgment means that you temporarily set aside the judgmental side of you. You may ask how this is possible if your judgments have been "normal" for as long as you can remember. It's not as difficult as you might imagine, and there are two techniques from which to choose. The first is the "mindset option." With this approach, you deliberately and with intention say to yourself, "I am going to set aside all possible judgments of my client for the next period of time (insert how long). I will do everything in my power to support my client, focus on his or her ultimate potential and capability, and hold my client and his or her wishes, dreams, and goals in the brightest light of possibility. It is my intention to use my power to help cause my client's success. I am here to serve, and I set aside my judgments." After the session is complete, you can have your judgments back if you truly want them.

The second method is the "judgment download." You take a pen and paper, or you can also enter the data on your computer. You capture every conceivable judgment that you have in your brain onto the paper (or computer). You then say to the data collection, "I am placing all of my judgments here for the time being, knowing that I can have them all back after the session is complete. I know they are safe and will not be forgotten, and whenever I want them, I know just where to find them. I now consciously release all of my judgments for this time period (insert time)."

CONNECTION

Connection is the most important aspect in every coaching session. Without connection, nothing happens. Judgments are the antithesis of connection. Judgments block connection, and connection overrides judgment. If you are judging the coachee, your connection has been broken. If you have a broken connection, stop and address it. Ask questions like: What just happened? Did I say something that upset you? Are you okay with me? If your connection is solid, then you are not judging the coachee. There are several steps to ensuring you are prepared and available to have a "static-free" connection. They are: becoming present, emptying your mind, letting go of being right, opening your heart, asking open-ended questions to establish the flow, and nurturing your childlike curiosity.

Become Present

Getting into the moment can be a simple process of taking several deep breaths, letting go of any stress, closing your eyes, and telling yourself, "I am here, at this moment, to serve and support another. I am consciously letting go of all other concerns, thoughts, tasks, people, and ideas. I am choosing to be 100 percent present for this time period (insert time allotted)." Memorize the three sentences and say them before every session.

Empty Your Mind

Before your client arrives, download your mind onto a piece of paper. This is different from a "judgment download" in that many of the things on your mind are tasks, thoughts and ideas, even feelings. Write them down as they enter your mind, in no specific order. Like the judgment download, you are asking the paper (or computer) to be a receptacle to hold what is on your mind until later when you can have it back. This process works effectively because your mind merely needs to know that these thoughts will not be forgotten.

Let Go of Being Right

Right and wrong are polarities. If one person is right, then the other must be wrong. There is no room for right and wrong in a coaching session. Coaching is like having an Earth angel who is there to support your dreams coming true. Angels aren't invested in being right or proving anyone wrong. When you find yourself invested in knowing the answers, telling or arguing that you are right, let it go. It doesn't matter if you are "right" in the session. No one is keeping score. Remember that <u>knowing and being right may have been useful in school,</u> but they are inappropriate in your coaching sessions. <u>Let go of knowing the answers for others</u> as well as the need to be right.

Open Your Heart

As you do more work with your chakras, you will become more comfortable with your different energy centers (see Chapter 6). Opening your heart happens with three simple steps. First, close your eyes. Second, take three deep breaths, and let go of any tension with each breath you exhale. Third, picture in your mind's eye someone you deeply and dearly love and with whom you feel gratitude. It can be a child, a parent, a spouse, a sister, or a dear friend. It must be someone with whom you experience a sort of "melting sensation" in your chest; softness is added to your demeanor, and a dewy sensation occurs around your eyes. We refer to these physical sensations as indicators of unconditional love. After you have done those three things, your heart will definitely be open.

Ask Open-Ended Questions to Establish the Flow

When you ask closed-ended questions, the client answers either "yes" or "no," and the conversation ends right there. Closed-ended questions stop the flow of energy. Open-ended questions invite the flow of energy and initiate the conversation because you cannot simply say "yes" or "no" to any of the questions. Open-ended questions sound like this: What is your objective? Can you give me an example? Tell me more about that.

Where do you want to go from here? Can you elaborate on that? What happened just before that feeling? What was the experience like? These types of open-ended questions will open the flow of energy so that your client can speak freely to you. In your coaching journal, keep a list of open-ended questions, and practice using them in your sessions. Notice when you use closed questions, and notice the closed response.

Allow Your Childlike Curiosity

Children are naturally curious. They are eager to learn about the world, and they haven't learned yet to edit their questions. They ask questions with an open mind, ready to learn from the conversation. Find that childlike part of you. Open up to the purity and transparency that you possess. Allow the "not knowing" simple and honest questions of the child in you to come forward. Then listen with the innocence of the child who lives within you. Allow your innate curiosity to surface and be present. Your curiosity is your greatest asset in coaching. Curiosity and focus will enable you to keep your attention on your coachee and will naturally quiet the mind.

THE QUIET MIND

Having a quiet mind means that when you are still, you hear nothing. There is silence between your ears, absence of mind chatter, and you can listen to the stillness in the space around you. You can listen to your inner voice, and you can hear your client easily. This is the reason that having a quiet mind is so important for you as a coach. There are varying degrees of mind chatter that range from a few offhanded comments to non-stop dialogue. Depending upon the activity in your mind at the time, you will select the technique that will work for your current situation.

Techniques to Quiet the Mind and Uplift the Spirit

Be physical. If your mind is overactive, physical activity helps stop the chatter. When you engage in physical activity, it is difficult for the mind to engage. The more aerobic the activity, the less chance your mind has to chatter at you. Dancing, skipping, running, and jumping on a "rebounder" all create a positive effect to silence the voices in your head when they attempt to engage. Do something every day for at least twenty minutes to quiet and manage your mental voices.

Be still and tune in to yourself. When you have overscheduled your agenda, quieting your mind entails stopping everything. When you are quiet, you get to hear the rhythm of your soul. Find time each day to listen to your spirit. Find time to be still and drink in the silence. Find time to tune in to your essence and honor who you are. It is in the stillness that you will connect with your spiritual DNA, your inner compass, your metaphysical GPS. Turn off the noise of the world, be peaceful and quiet, and connect with yourself.

Read inspirational quotes. If you start to question your choices and second-guess yourself, words of inspiration can help reassure you. In your coaching journal, gather all of your favorite quotes. Collect them as if they were precious jewels to be treasured. In your quiet time, read them and let their wisdom trickle over you, uplifting your spirit.

Listen to special music. There are many ways to recharge your spirit. One of them is to listen to music that touches a deep chord inside you. Music is a personal experience, so there isn't a universal list of compositions that will inspire you. When you discover music that connects to the deepest part of you, capture the name in your coaching journal. When you have time, download it to your computer and load it in your musical companion. Keep music with you to shift the energy whenever you need a lift. You can also recharge your spirit with your other four senses. Make sure you are discriminating when you choose what refuels you.

LISTENING TO YOUR INNER MESSAGES

A message is an inner imperative to do something that stretches you outside of your comfort zone. Messages are your inner guidance asking you to do something that is irrational, illogical, unreasonable, and not within your plan. Messages stretch you beyond your comfort zone by asking you to do something that you don't normally do. When you are coaching, you will notice messages come to you, urging you to say or do something out of the ordinary. <u>If a message comes to you three times in a row, pay attention</u>, because it will persist until you do what is being requested. Your clients will also receive messages. If you listen to, trust, and act on your messages, so will your clients. The messages are very important to the coaching process.

After you have quieted the voices of your mind, you will then be able to hear the messages of the soul. These gentle whispers are guidance from your higher self as to what is next in your spiritual evolution. The messages come in a variety of forms: flashes of insight, synchronistic happenings, images, words in the form of tasks to be done, and suggestions from people who dearly care about you. Depending on your comfort with the spiritual side of life, you might allocate the origin of messages to a higher power, angels, or a loved one who has transitioned. The essential thing about messages is that you will be inconvenienced by what they say, and you won't want to follow what they ask. When you listen to your irrational, illogical, and unreasonable messages, you will tune in to that spiritual guidance that we invoke in a coaching session. As you practice this in your life, you will become more comfortable with the intuitive part of yourself. Then when you receive messages in a coaching session, you will be ready, willing, and able to listen to them because you will be more accustomed to the message process. Messages can only be heard when you are still and listening to the whispers of your inner knowing.

⚜

Listening with a quiet mind enables you to recreate another person's reality. When you learn to listen to the silence within you, you can tune in to the universal rhythm. Coaching is the connection of two souls in the magic of the void. The essence of the coaching session is best captured in a song from the musical *The Last Sweet Days of Isaac*: "A transparent crystal moment when your life is suspended like a dewdrop in the spiderweb of time and space." This is the essence of the coaching session.

Choices and Decisions

"If you don't like something, change it. If you can't change it, change your attitude. Don't complain."

Maya Angelou

*L*ife is a series of choices. From the moment you wake up each day to the moment you go to sleep, you must make choices. You need to determine what to eat, what to wear, where to go, what to do, what to remember. Your day is a series of options and choices. From moment to moment, you must sort out how to use your time, how to establish your priorities, and how to align your energy and motivation with the time available. Each day you will make hundreds of choices and decisions about what will and won't get done. The process of choosing is not new, but the complexity of our lives multiplies exponentially the amount of choices that we face and exacerbates the pressure to make the "right" choices. When you coach another, you must both understand why making these choices becomes difficult, and you must empathize with the nature of the choices confronting your client. <u>One of the most important aspects of becoming an empowering coach is to have had the personal experience of being supported by another in making complex choices and in overcoming adversity.</u>

As a coach, your job is to help your clients make choices regarding their challenges from an inner-directed, mindful place. When your clients reach a crossroad, are offered opportunities with various ramifications, or have reached a critical point in their evolution, <u>your purpose is to help them access their deepest reservoir of inner knowing and support them</u> on their path to their destination. Your encouraging caring, without agenda, will provide the oasis they seek in order to sort out the issues and lessons they face. <u>Helping them to find their internal compass</u>, aligning their course of action, and supporting them on their journeys is your job description.

Greg was newly married and had a newborn son. He had been experiencing some difficulties in his marriage, and his company was also lacking clients. In his dilemma, he didn't know whether to focus on his marriage or his work. He found himself feeling ineffective, confused, and stuck. He never anticipated that he would end up in this type of situation. His wife had gone to visit her relatives in South America, while he was working in Europe and considering a job in the United States. The complex situation not only involved a shaky marriage, an uncertain business, and a newborn, but it also involved multiple residential options on different continents. In the coaching session, we addressed all the various scenarios that could possibly unfold. Then I asked about his highest priority. His response focused on his relationship with his wife and child. As we explored options, he showed energy and enthusiasm when he could create a whole new set of circumstances. The outcome of the session wasn't "option A," staying in Europe or "option B," moving to the United States, but rather a new possibility, "option C," exploring the opportunities in South America, which would please his wife, make him feel empowered, and put him back in the driver's seat of his life. He chose an option that made his eyes twinkle because it included his preferences: adventure, freedom, and personal power.

What happens in the process of sorting out options and determining what action you must take? What must be considered when you examine your options and select your preference? What happens internally when you feel stuck and cannot make a choice? What can coaches do to help their clients get unstuck and feel confident with their choices? Let's explore the anatomy of choice and decision. When do you make a choice, and when do you make a decision?

THE ANATOMY OF CHOICE AND DECISION

As noted in Chapter 2, the definition of choice is "to select freely that which you want from a series of alternatives." A decision, on the other hand, is "a conclusion or a determination about something that is based on rational, logical, and reasonable facts and information." Choices are intuitive, driven by preferences, satisfying to the self, feel right, and can stretch you outside your comfort zone. Decisions are rational, driven by expectations, appease others, often justified with reasons and explanations, and don't necessarily require a stretch.

When we compare decisions and choices, we see that a decision is rational, whereas a choice is intuitive. A decision is logical and reasonable, whereas a choice feels right on a gut level. A decision can be explained by reasons, whereas a choice is based on personal preference. A decision is driven by external expectations, whereas a choice is driven by intrinsic proclivity. A decision appeases others, whereas a choice is satisfying to the self. A decision is comfortable, whereas a choice can be uncomfortable.

The conditions for making a *choice* are: There is either a statement of dissatisfaction with the status quo, or there is an expression of desire for something different from what currently exists. The person examines what he or she feels about the situation, explores what he or she ideally wants. The various options are reviewed, preferences are articulated, and the person selects the most desirable option. Finally, the person commits to his or her choice. Choices are intrinsically initiated and, when this progression is followed, the person making the choice experiences satisfaction and fulfillment.

Jim is offered a job opportunity, and from the description it immediately sounds like a match for his capabilities and his lifestyle. He becomes enthusiastic, explores the expectations, requirements, and compensation, and because of his excitement, he jumps at the opportunity. The choice is made based on the energy and motivation that Jim experiences. This is a clear *choice*.

The conditions for making a *decision* look like this: There is a situation that requires resolution. The person examines his or her expectations and the ramifications and consequences of each option. A decision is made based on those criteria or the "shoulds." The outcome often results in reservations rather than a clear commitment, and the person who is deciding may end up feeling less than satisfied with the outcome.

A job is offered to Anna, and she weighs the opportunity, the financial compensation, the potential for advancement, the expectations in terms of hours on the job, the commute, the restraints and freedoms, the impact on her personal and family life, and the impact on her résumé. She discusses the prospect with her husband and gives the new job consideration. The decision will be made based on logic, rational thought, and the sensibleness to their family situation. This is a *decision*.

The two models look like this:

Should	**Want**
Decision	**Choice**
Reservations	**Commitment**

Both Anna and Jim have different styles in determining their course of action. Neither scenario is "right"; however, when commitment is solidly in place, there is more incentive and enthusiasm to pursue the plan than merely doing the "sensible" thing. Research has demonstrated that following one's preferences leads to more long-range and fulfilling outcomes.

People who tend to operate cognitively are usually more comfortable making decisions. People who operate affectively (from their emotions) are more comfortable making choices. Both types of people are capable of making both decisions and choices; however, many people hesitate to make either one. The question that most coaches must face is why people are indecisive.

WHY PEOPLE ARE INDECISIVE

When people are indecisive, they are afraid of making a mistake and reaping adverse consequences that might result from their error in judgment. They are afraid of a negative outcome, the ensuing self-criticism, and the potential judgments of others. Fear becomes the central motivator. Fear helps them avoid the potential adverse consequences of loss of affection, recognition, validation, and love. They decide to do what will be less risky for them, rather than doing what resonates. When people are indecisive, they will often say, "I don't know what I want," which really means, "I am afraid to know, because if I do know what I want, I will have to take action and actually do something." Between their "I don't knows" and their "I knows" are four layers: confusion, doubt, uncertainty, and fear. When people say, "I don't know," they don't commit to anything; they stay on the "I don't know" fence and avoid making a mistake by not choosing the perceived "wrong" item. They protect themselves by staying in the safety zone. As long as they stay in their comfort zone, in familiar surroundings, with no increased demands, with predictable expectations that they can meet, with little disruption, they will not activate the "I can't" side of their minds. However, as soon as they move into the stretch zone, put themselves in unfamiliar surroundings, take on the challenge of learning something totally new with high expectations, unpredictability, and a considerable amount of disruption, the "I can'ts" will certainly begin to surface.

When you say, "I can't," it is symptomatic of a condition that we have labeled "negaholism." Negaholism is about focusing on the negative and reinforcing it right up to the level of self-sabotage. We have written an entire book on negaholism, which is a large topic and quite involved. When people are unable to make choices, they talk themselves out of what they want either because they don't believe they can have it, or because they are hard on themselves for any preference they indicate. Beating themselves up keeps them safe in indecision, because sitting on the "I don't know what to do" fence is uncommitted to any choice.

Each one of us has certain standards we establish for ourselves. The standards are based on past experiences. When we have a situation that does not match up with our concept of ourselves, it creates a schism between our idea of who we are and the reality of the situation. We call this the "margin for beat-up." It is the discrepancy between what you anticipate and the reality of the situation that creates this division.

For example, you establish a standard for yourself that states you are an organized person. As you are leaving your house for a business trip, you accidentally forget the envelope with the tax payment that must be mailed overnight today. You don't realize it until you are on the plane, having your final cell-phone conversation with your spouse in another country, who says, "You did remember to mail the taxes, didn't you?" This moment is a behavioral crossroads. You know that you blew it and haven't lived up to your expectations of yourself. The crossroads you are presented with means that you can either use your present circumstances against yourself, or you can somehow solve the problem without taking yourself to task. If you opt to flog yourself for your actions, you embark on a "negattack." A negattack is an attack against yourself and is a symptom of negaholism. You berate yourself for not living up to the expectations and standards you previously established for yourself—that you are an organized person who remembers important tasks.

NEGAHOLISM

Negaholism is the separation between your essential self and your ego (your perception of your worth). The condition engages when you feel stressed or overwhelmed, and something happens that triggers a hostile conversation with yourself whereby the ego starts attacking the self. In the situation with your spouse, when you realize that you forgot to mail the taxes as you had agreed to do, you probably feel guilt, regret, remorse, and disappointment. You take yourself to task for all the counterproductive actions that have caused you embarrassment and humiliation. You discover that part of you is engaged in behavior that is counterproductive to your expectations, behaviors, and goals. The feelings of embarrassment consequently lead to a negattack. The negattack evokes feelings of insecurity, inadequacy, and the inability to perform or deliver what is requested at the time. The negattack compounds the situation. Not only have you done something that does not live up to your expectations, that lets other people down and makes you feel guilty, but the self-flagellation, in effect, rubs your nose in it, and makes you feel worthless. The overwhelming feeling focuses on the "disaster" that you have caused through your forgetfulness. You now engage in a downward corkscrew globalizing the situation with conclusions like, "I never do anything right." This adds insult to injury, and your self-esteem starts to plummet. This creates a separation within you; your essential self did something while your ego observed in disbelief.

With all these feelings comes the desire to find some relief in order to function. The inclination is to mask, suppress, or replace the feelings of insufficiency with a temporary fix or "feel good" moment (using a cigarette, a cup of coffee, something sweet, TV, shopping, a drink, a drug, and so on), substituting a substance, an experience, or a process for the mental torment. The "fix" is selected to distract from the pain of overwhelming worthlessness and inadequacy, and to provide temporary relief. This short-term gratification eventually wears off, and the feelings of anxiety, apprehension, and fear regarding the situation eventually return. The cycle repeats itself over and over again until it becomes "normal" to you to mask the feelings with a substance, an experience, or a process. With repetition, this cycle becomes habitual and eventually can become an addiction.

Here are four examples of situations that might cause a negattack: (1) You are preparing for a presentation, and you procrastinate. At the eleventh hour, you panic with all you have to do and the short amount of time remaining. You have a negattack. (2) You're on a restrictive eating program, and you act out by eating something that is not on the program. You have a negattack. (3) You have an important meeting. You wake up late, get stuck in traffic, speed to compensate, get a traffic ticket on the way, and arrive significantly late for the meeting. You have a negattack. (4) You draw a bubble bath and set up the battery-operated DVD player so you can watch a movie at the same time. As you are relaxing in the tub, the cat jumps up on the table where you have the DVD player, knocks it into the tub, and it becomes submerged. The DVD machine is ruined, and so is your relaxing bath. The result is that you have a negattack. List situations in which you do not live up to your expectations of yourself.

Negattacks occur to intelligent, talented, and capable people for very specific reasons. When you have a negattack, you beat yourself up, and as a result you create a *triple imprint* in your behavior. The triple imprint involves psychological, emotional, and physiological aspects. The psychological imprint comes from the *attention* you get from yourself and others for the behavior you exhibited. The emotional imprint comes from the *dramatic* situation and the feelings associated with the negattack. The physiological imprint is the *chemical rush* that is released into your system from the attacking of a substandard behavior.

The psychological reinforcement occurs when people are in an environment in which positive recognition, reinforcement, and rewards are withheld. Without any possibility of positive attention, they gravitate to the only other attention option, negative attention (since being ignored is not a viable alternative).

The emotional reinforcement comes from the drama. The protagonist and the antagonist create an internal conflict inflicted on the self from the mental berating of not living up to expectations, causing diminishment, disconnection, and tension. The drama is exciting and emotionally charged. The juxtaposition of the painful feeling caused by the anxiety coupled with the exciting feelings caused by the drama contribute to the perplexity of the situation.

The physiological reinforcement comes from substances called opiate peptides that are released into your system. Opiate peptides have the opposite effect of endorphins. Opiate peptides, a string of amino acids, create a chemical rush in your system that locks in the addictive pattern. Opiate peptides stress your neuroendocrine system, attack your immune system, and make you more susceptible to illness. (If you want to know more about this condition, read *Negaholics: How to Overcome Negativity and Turn Your Life Around.*)

Bella, a client, asked me for a session in overcoming her "I can'ts," and I enthusiastically agreed. Bella is a scientist who often attacks herself for her limitations that block her enjoyment of life. When asked a simple question like, "What would you like to eat?" she replies, "I don't know," triggering her internal conversation between what she would like and what she can have. Bella has extensive food allergies and restrictions, and as a result says "I can't" to many situations in which she would really love to participate. She can't eat sugar, wheat, dairy, or meat. She needs to eat fruit in small quantities, and vegetables are the staple in her diet. Although she dutifully follows this regime, she isn't happy about it. The session was about Bella coming to a choice about her condition. As the session progressed, it seemed like a grim life sentence of no-fun food. I finally asked her, "Are there no fun moments around food?" She replied, "Tea time is my favorite time!" I asked, "What happens at tea time?" Her face lit up, and she started her animated narrative, "At tea time, I get to be the queen. Everyone gathers, and I make a huge pot of tea, and I am the center of attention." I looked puzzled, "What do you eat?" She looked delighted and said, "I get to eat an entire package of spelt cookies!" I commented that she must like them because of the glint in her eyes. She said, "It is the only time when I feel normal." I proceeded to ask her what other situations she could create that would enable her to feel this same way. She thought and said, "I need to think about this because right now tea time is the only one." One by one, her imagination started to yield new ideas that would allow her to feel free from all of the food restrictions that were governing her life. Some were related to food, but others were about breaking self-imposed rules that would give her a sense of liberation. Bella was a very strict person, and giving herself permission to break some of her "rules" freed her from her restrictive food prison. She left the session delighted with her newfound solutions.

IMPRINTS

In order for people to take back their power, and to become senior to their challenges and issues, they need to create positive imprints that alter the way they perceive their situation. This is also a way to help people overcome indecision.

An imprint is something that makes a significant impression that lasts a very long time. Imprints have both emotional and psychological components, and they may also have a physiological component. Negative imprints can happen to you as a child, for example, when you are teased or bullied in middle school, or as an adult, such as when you are invalidated. But you can also create your own positive imprints. The way you do this is to:

1. Determine your outcome.
2. Formulate your list of significant emotional triggers.
3. List the people who need to be included.
4. List props or clothes to make the imprint more real.
5. Design your method to positively imprint yourself now and for your future.

6. Do the ritual, process, exercise or rite of passage that will allow you to create your personal positive imprints.

If you need support from those close to you, ask for it. People are usually ready, willing, and able to lend support to a friend who asks for it. Using your creativity to positively imprint your beliefs and behaviors and reality will significantly alter, if not completely replace, the old patterns.

In order for people to make a choice about a concern in their life, they need to trust themselves. For them to trust themselves, they need to know that whatever choice they make will ultimately be the perfect choice for them to learn whatever lesson they need to learn. They also must forgive themselves for "mistakes" or perceived mistakes from the past that are used as evidence to mistrust themselves, and avoid making choices and embarking on new endeavors. For many people, forgiveness is a concept they find difficult to implement. Forgiveness appears to be something outside of them, especially when it comes to forgiving themselves. In order for them to forgive themselves for past mistakes or heal the past traumas that have been imprinted, they must engage in a process that involves four steps: (1) release, (2) repair, (3) reconcile, and (4) reconnect. This four-step process will help unlock the old imprint from their system, heal the old wounds, and enable them to have a new beginning freed from the issue.

Release

The purpose of releasing energy is to unlock the molecules of emotion that have locked the pattern of behavior in place. Release is a literal experience. Aristotle addressed "bringing to the surface repressed emotions, complexes, and feelings in an effort to identify and relieve them through theatre, especially tragedy which results in release and purification." The emotions are purified through the evocation of intense fear, empathy, and pity. When you release energy related to an unresolved issue, you can feel it with every part of you. Releasing energy takes many different forms: tears, anger, rage, laughter, dancing, singing, yelling, screaming, hitting, kicking, pounding, pushing, or punching. The form you choose should be appropriate to the experience and the emotions from the past that you want to release. Most people are uncomfortable at first with the thought of fully expressing emotions and releasing the energy that is associated with the imprinted past experience. They would prefer to hope it away, meditate it away, or through love and light have it magically vaporize. The reality of healing past incidents is that it is a four-step process that must be conducted in sequence.

The process works like this: You take an unresolved incident from the past in which you felt diminished, discounted, discarded, or denied. You recall the incident as vividly as you can, and you examine your feelings. You allow those feelings to bubble to the surface, to be reexperienced, and then released with you appearing as your most powerful and best self.

You ask yourself what it would take to regain your self-respect, reclaim your right to be heard and seen, and to experience your dignity. Ask yourself who needs to hear you express your truth. Determine what words need to be said in order to release you from the shackles of the past. Decide what you need to do. You then set up a safe environment with supportive, nonjudgmental people who won't take anything personally. At that point, you externalize the hurt, loss, sadness, unfulfilled expectations, and outrage, and give yourself permission to fully and safely express and release in words, actions, and sounds to remove the old trauma from your system and free you from the past. When you are successful, you will experience a huge *release* of energy coupled with relief.

Repair

After the release of energy is complete, you can then begin to *repair*. Repair or healing happens only after release. To repair means to make whole, to restore, or to rectify something that caused discord, animosity, or a painful affliction. After repair is complete, the reconciliation can begin.

Reconcile

Reconciliation or forgiveness will most likely be toward yourself and the person involved in the incident. Forgiveness is the erasing of an emotional debt. Forgiveness means that you give thanks to the universe "for giving" you the lesson that gave you back a part of yourself.

Reconnect

Reconnection is the culmination of the cycle. Reconnection happens when the other stages are complete. Think of the wound from the past like a bee sting. First, you must remove the stinger; that is the release. Then you must remove any venom associated with the wound. That starts the healing, which is about repair. Forgiveness or reconciliation will erase the experience. Finally, when all is healed, you can then reconnect with yourself and/or the other person involved in the incident.

These steps must occur in sequence. You cannot repair before you have released the energy. You cannot reconnect before you have reconciled the original incident.

If you haven't healed the past, it is difficult to choose about the future. Choosing is the active process of designing your future, both short-term and long-term. The whole purpose of the four-step process is to release old imprints, and then to create new imprints for your future. Imprints work hand-in-hand with your beliefs that drive your behaviors. This progression from hurt to healing and beyond enables you to release the past and to make new choices in your life. You no longer need to have the future dictated by any past incidents because you have successfully removed them from your emotional reservoir.

BELIEFS

Beliefs dictate reality and create self-fulfilling prophecies. Beliefs emanate from either concepts or repeated experiences. When you form conscious or unconscious beliefs, you give them power to cause your reality. In addition, you unconsciously look for evidence in your life that validates and confirms your beliefs. Beliefs are so powerful that they magnetize reality to line up and conform to the belief. Some examples of beliefs are: *I can't function without coffee. If I don't have eight hours of sleep, I am useless. I am terrible with numbers. I always attract the wrong men. I never win anything. Bad things always happen to me.* As a coach, if you hear a repeating, self-defeating belief, you need to gently point it out to your coachee. If the coachee has unconscious beliefs that are counterproductive, he or she must first be aware of them before setting out to dismantle them; otherwise, whatever work you do together will be an uphill battle fighting against your coachee's beliefs. Some questions you want to ask are: Do you hear that you have this belief? Do you want to keep this belief? Do you want the outcomes that this belief produces? Do you want to change this belief? What new belief do you want to replace the old belief with? If coachees want to change their beliefs, they need to follow the five steps to dismantling old beliefs that don't serve you. The five steps are:

1. Become aware of what your beliefs are.
2. Articulate the new belief that you want to replace the old one.
3. Consciously search for evidence to confirm the new reality.
4. Build the case for your new belief.
5. Visualize the new belief working.

Let's take the belief, "I can't function without coffee," as an example. Are you aware that you have this belief? Do you want to keep it or change it? What new belief do you want to replace it with? The answer might be, "I wake up energetic with all the energy I need." Each morning when you awaken, you then look for evidence to validate your belief. With each day, you consciously build the case for your new belief. Finally, you see yourself in your meditations as an alert, fully energized, caffeine-free person.

Ways to Change Reality

Transitions are essential to personal evolution. The formalizing of transitions creates imprints that make your new reality true and momentous. Letting go of the old history and embracing your new reality is all part of the evolutionary process. As a coach, you need to be creative and think out of the box. You must encourage your coachees to break through old habits and behaviors in order to embark on new levels, dimensions, and chapters in their lives. Ultimately, what you do with each client is to help him make choices that he feels centered and excited about.

There are times in your coaching practice when you need to deviate from the traditional format of the session and employ activities to help your clients become "unstuck," allowing them to form new imprints or create new belief systems, which ultimately allows them to make their choices. These activities are usually employed after you have met with the client for several sessions and it has become evident that something is stuck on the molecular level. These activities include: processes, simulations, rituals, rites of passage, and assignments. We have conducted Inner Negotiation Workshops (INW) since 1976 in which we support people rearranging their behaviors through creating their own rites of passage, rituals, simulations, and processes to formulate their new desired imprints. If access to an INW is not possible, here are some options for you to consider using on your own.

Processes

A process is an activity that is directed toward a specific outcome that changes someone's reality. A process is something that rearranges cells that have been lodged in place through strong emotional connection. For instance, if your client has few or no boundaries and can't say "no," a process might be the perfect strategy to enable them to change their old way of behaving that has become ingrained. The process would involve requests to which the coachee practices saying "no." You could be the person making the requests, and the coachee would need to continually say "no." Or a process could involve your client practicing asking for support. The client would need to formulate the words, list the people with whom he or she holds back, and determine the appropriate request. Another situation might be breaking through an old pattern, such as giving reasons and excuses for behaviors.

Tina started to listen to her mind chatter: "Yeah, but you're too old. Yeah, but you're not smart enough. Yeah, but you don't have the education you need," and so on. She wanted to break out of the cycle of talking herself out of her dreams, and so she created a process. Her process involved putting herself into a corrugated box that she labeled with all of her "yeah, buts," and having the box taped shut. She wanted to break out of the box in a dramatic way so she would imprint on herself that she could do whatever she wanted. (We set it up with the word *stop* as her signal to open the box.) She did break out of the box, literally, and felt incredible power in overcoming her self-defeating, limiting beliefs. The process was so successful that her "yeah, but" voices were actually silenced.

A process can be used whenever someone needs to practice a new behavior. If a woman keeps getting passed over and she needs to take a stand, she might need to raise her voice to be heard. She might need to hear her own voice. There are a variety of situations in which a person needs to practice a new behavior. This practice is similar to learning a new language. You practice saying the unfamiliar words over and over again until they feel comfortable, natural, like they are part of you. This practice reinforces a new behavior and makes the new uncomfortable behavior more familiar and easier to embrace. When the person returns to her old environment, she has the new behavior available in her repertoire.

Simulations

A simulation is the re-creation of an incident that feels so real that it brings up the same emotions that the real experience once did. As I wrote earlier, both my husband and I are now pilots. After I became a pilot, I asked him to take a short course on landing the plane in case something happened to incapacitate me. He received his private pilot's license, and while he was in flight school, he cured himself of motion sickness and went on to become an instrument-rated pilot. We liken the simulation exercise to training pilots. When pilots are trained to fly more complex aircraft, they are often trained on a simulator. The simulator recreates the experience of a 747 or 777, without putting the pilot, passengers, or the aircraft at risk. The training can simulate adverse or emergency conditions to help the pilot see how he or she will react in an emergency. Then the correct response is practiced so that if a real emergency were to occur, the pilot would have the behavior that would be required already established in his emergency response system.

For example, Tom, a participant in an Inner Negotiation Workshop, had difficulty confronting retail clerks when he wanted to return a product that was unsatisfactory. A recent incident that intimidated Tom was at the tire store. Tom was reticent about returning the substandard tires that he bought for his truck because he was uncomfortable confronting the sales clerk. Tom chose the most intimidating man in the workshop to play the role of the clerk, and then created a simulation of the real situation that brought up all the emotions from his original incident. He practiced the simulation over and over again until he felt confident about his ability to confront his discomfort and fear. The purpose of the simulation is to recreate reality so closely that the same feelings resurface. When Tom actually returned the tires to the store where he purchased them and communicated his displeasure, to his surprise he received a full refund without any confrontation. He had the opportunity to actually try on and simulate the new behavior ahead of time, in a safe environment, so that he felt confident enough to do it in real life in the actual store. To say the least, Tom had a breakthrough and was truly delighted with the outcome. If you say, "That's playacting and wouldn't work for me," then watch a powerful drama like 24 and see if you get an adrenaline rush. You know it is a TV show, and you know the people are actors, but it is so real and so well done that you become immersed in the action. This is similar to what simulation can do for you in a positive and productive manner. Get the right people to take the simulation seriously, allow yourself to get drawn into the drama, and you will also be able to rearrange the molecules and have a significant breakthrough. Molecules of emotion become established when something significant happens. When you alter your reality, you literally change the old molecules associated with the emotion. Dr. Candace Pert, an internationally renowned psychopharmacologist and author of two books, *Molecules of Emotion* and *Everything You Need to Know to Feel Good,* validates the MMS approach to emotions. She says that all feelings are a natural part of our physiology, and as such shouldn't be divided into good feelings and bad feelings. There are no "bad" emotions, but rather unexpressed emotions that are the result of suppression and denial. When feelings are suppressed, the information molecules become blocked at the cellular receptors, impeding the free flow of important functions throughout the psychosomatic network. When doing simulations with a coachee, always create a "safety" in case the original feelings surface in full expression.

Rituals

A ritual is a special ceremony created specifically to imprint on those present that something has officially transpired. Rituals usually include actions, words, special attire, and possibly music. The ritual can be a single event or it can be repeated; however, it is conducted in a rather official and formal manner. Rituals involve conferring of status, transitioning from one state to another, or changing a life condition.

Eleanor wanted to stop smoking. She had tried it on her own and failed. She had gone to clinics and joined groups, but nothing seemed to work. Finally, in a session with her coach, she determined to design a ritual in which she would declare that she had officially stopped smoking forever. She gathered some friends together and lit up as many cigarettes as she could hold in her mouth. She inhaled and almost got sick. This imprint was so vivid that Eleanor said, "That is the end!" The ritual she created to end an old habit finally worked for her.

Rites of Passage

A rite of passage is a public event that marks a significant transition in a person's life. In our society we have certain rites of passage. Some of them are births, christenings, bar mitzvahs, graduations, weddings, funerals, and so on. These events are used as markers to imprint that something significant has changed a person's life and status in a meaningful way.

Sam took the Inner Negotiation Workshop, and one of his objectives was to transition into manhood. Although he was thirty-five, he still had many boyish traits. He wanted to become a man, but he had received so much reinforcement about what a "cute kid" he was that he seemed to cling to his boyish qualities. In the workshop, Sam designed his rite of passage from boyhood to manhood. He asked for witnesses to help him etch the event in his psyche. He chose the clothing to signify the change, the words that conveyed the meaning, the music and the symbols that represented his transition. He designed and executed his rite of passage that marked for him his entry into adult manhood, something that he will never forget.

Assignments

There are times when you, the coach, will give assignments to your coachee that must be completed before the next session. These assignments must always be in alignment with the focus and purpose of the session. For example, if the session is about securing a new job, the assignment might be about researching opportunities or perhaps interviewing successful people in the industry. If the session is about time management, you might give the assignment for the coachee to keep a log of how he or she currently allocates time.

In addition, there are exercises that you might propose to your clients.

If you are doing a relationship session with someone who wants to create a relationship, you might have the coachee complete the exercises in the first three chapters of *If Love Is a Game, These Are the Rules.* If you are working with a client on customer service, you may assign the project of documenting three outstanding customer-service experiences to share with you at the next session. When you give reading assignments, written exercises, or research assignments, you encourage clients to engage, to take initiative and responsibility for their own progress and results. Giving relevant assignments is one of the ways to engage coachees in their own process.

Choices and decisions are both similar and different. To be an effective coach, you need to know the types of people you are dealing with, and understand and respect their preferred style. It also helps to have a variety of options available for them to change habits, try on new behaviors, and transition into their new life. As the coach, you open up the doors of possibility, help your coachees envision their preferred situation, and support them in making it happen.

*A*rticulating Objectives and Manifesting Reality

"Faith is to believe what you do not yet see;
the reward for this faith is to see what you believe."
St. Augustine

*A*ttracting what you want like a magnet requires information, intention, attention, and the willingness to do what is required. It acts like the gravitational pull of the Earth. Once you know how to function like gravity, you will begin to manifest your heart's desires without fear of your own power.

THE TEN STEPS TO ATTRACT WHAT YOU WANT

Attracting what you want requires ten steps: (1) make a clear statement of what you want, (2) make the request; feel and visualize it becoming your reality, (3) take action and do what is required, (4) become and remain unattached to the outcome, (5) be willing for the outcome to surface in its own unique way, (6) believe that what you want is possible, (7) hold it lightly, (8) have an attitude of gratitude, (9) become the clear channel, eliminating all static that could block connection to universal giving, and (10) be grateful, humble, and generous with your manifestations. The following elaborates each of these steps:

1. **Make a clear statement of what you want.** In the coaching process, we call this an objective. Desire is wanting. You have to be willing to want something that is not presently part of your reality. Desire requires a certain amount of truth telling, admitting to yourself that you want something new and different. Will's objective was to become "thin Will." He had tried to alter his weight in the past and was successful up to a point, but then when the goal was close to being accomplished, he would relapse back to where he was originally or gain even more weight. His mental picture and his actual weight were not a match, and this made him very uncomfortable in his body. Will's first step in the process was to state clearly that he wanted to become thirty pounds lighter by a reasonable and realistic date. In stating the objective, we deliberately avoided using the word "lose," since there is a negative connotation associated with losing anything (losing your keys, losing your wallet, losing your mind). The target date was important because the goal needs to be something the coachee can believe is possible in the time frame allotted.

2. **Make your request and visualize it happening.** Will had to communicate with his coach the intention and the goal date. He had to see if his coach could also agree that the goal was possible in the time allotted. The coach had to see if the intention and goal were supportable in the projected time frame. If the coach feels that the goal is too ambitious or unrealistic, it is necessary to communicate this to the coachee. Both coach and coachee must agree on the goal, the goal date, the strategy, the support, and the consequences if the plan fails or is aborted. This is called a *coaching contract*. This contract can be verbal; however, it is always better to have every-

thing documented because people can easily forget. If the contract is documented, and both people have copies, then any confusion over the agreement can be checked with the documents. Will must be willing and able to sign the contract, knowing full well that it is up to him to cause his desired result to happen. The coach is there to monitor progress, to address recidivism, and to acknowledge and celebrate successes. Will must also visualize his goal happening. Visualizing is so important because the mental imprint will magnetize to you what you envision. Will must see himself as the thin man he wants to become and feel the feelings associated with "thinness." He can locate a photo of himself as a thin, younger man or get a computer-generated image of himself to post in key places in his home, his car, and his workplace to reinforce his image of himself as thin and fit. Or he can meditate and see the image in his mind's eye: Will, the thin man.

3. **Take action and do what is required.** In order to take action, you must have a plan. The plan is what will get you from here to there. Willingness means that you are willing to do whatever you need to do to make the desired change happen. If you are willing, it means you are open to creating solutions. If you are willing, you don't talk yourself out of what you want because it is a stretch for you. Instead, you embark on the journey to fulfillment with an attitude of embracing what life offers you. Even though there are many ways to reach an outcome, there is not necessarily a "best" way to eliminate undesirable weight. There is, however, a way that the coachee will choose and is willing to commit to and stick with. It is up to the coach to help the coachee find that plan and stay the course. Support and regular check-in points are essential for the coachee to stay on track. Whether the program is about calories, carbohydrates, fat, exercise, portion control, fasting, capsules, or colonics, Will must choose the program, believe it will work for him, cause it to work, and work the plan.

4. **Remain unattached to the outcome.** Attachment to the outcome is where many people fail. Their identity becomes so invested in the future expectation that they believe they will be inadequate if their goal is not achieved. In other words, if they don't succeed, they will label themselves losers. This pressure impedes progress and can sabotage the entire mission. Unattachment means that you are not heavily invested in the outcome. When you are unattached, you know in the core of your being that you are sufficient without any changes, additions, or deletions. You allow the object of your desire to come to you without any force, pressure, or control. Unattachment means that it is acceptable for the goal to manifest, and it is equally okay for the goal to abort. This means that Will must be okay with himself the way he is, while he is simultaneously committed to his goal. It is a paradox (where two seemingly opposite statements are true), but it is required for the outcome to be produced.

5. **Be willing for the outcome to surface.** For Will to reach his goal, he needs to allow the process to work. He can't overly control it; he must allow it. Part of his due diligence is getting to the root of the issue. Gaining, losing, and then gaining more weight than you started with is called "the rubber band" weight-loss process. We have watched celebrities do this process publicly for decades. Will needs to get to the cause of his overweight condition if he will ever conclusively solve this dilemma. He needs to look at why he eats, when he eats, what he eats, and what he can do to either heal the core issue or substitute other behaviors or substances.

6. **Believe that your request is possible.** Belief means that you believe it is possible for you to have the object you desire. You can envision it. You can see yourself with it in your world. You can feel what it is like to have it. Belief also means you believe in yourself. Belief means you believe you are worthy of that which you desire. If Will doesn't believe his request is possible, then it isn't. If he thinks, "I

will do what I have to do, but I don't think it will work," he will
engage in self-sabotage that will derail the mission. His subcon-
scious will be saying, "I told you so," and it will eventually be right.
Even if everyone in his family has been fat for generations, he needs
to believe that he can break the chain; otherwise, he is doomed to
failure.

7. **Hold it lightly**. Throughout the process of becoming thin (his
physical authentic self), Will must monitor his thoughts and the
energy he has regarding winning or losing. If he has a great deal of
investment in losing, then he may be drawn to self-sabotaging
behaviors. If Will has a great deal of his focus on winning, he may
be drawn to succeeding. He may also flip back and forth between
winning one day and losing the next. His energy may be aligned
with his intentions, or it may sabotage his wishes. He also must
notice his thinking regarding becoming thin. Thoughts become
reality, and if Will's thoughts aren't in alignment with his intentions, he could have one foot on the accelerator and the other foot
on the brake.

8. **Have an attitude of gratitude.** Being grateful is your way to express
your humility and keep your ego from taking credit for your manifestations. When your ego takes the credit, you become arrogant.
Gratitude means that you sincerely appreciate what you receive. It
means that you receive at the level of your essence, transcending
your ego. Gratitude keeps you honest, authentic, and pure. When
you are grateful, you remain in a harmonious state. What you focus
on will multiply. If you focus on gratitude, you will increase your
blessings. However, you cannot have the motive to grow your blessings and therefore adopt the attitude of gratitude in order to create
abundance—it will backfire. You must be sincerely grateful for your
blessings, and not try to manipulate the universe by acting grateful.

9. **Become clear and remove all static to the source.** Becoming clear
means that you examine your conscience to ensure that your

motives are pure. It means that you unclutter yourself from anything that could be blocking your connection to universal abundance, as was discussed in Chapter 1. Examining your thoughts means that you reinforce all thoughts toward manifesting your desire. It means that you don't talk yourself out of your goal. You monitor any negative ideas that come to you and replace them with positive perceptions instead. Words are the way you communicate about your desire. If you downplay your desire because you don't want to appear arrogant, or you diminish your true desire because you are afraid that others might say you are engaged in self-sabotage, the universe will receive the message. The words you choose represent your internal reality and either reinforce or undercut your desires. Pay attention to the language you use to articulate your desire. In his innermost thoughts and words, Will needs to make sure that he isn't scheming to take revenge on all those who ridiculed him in the past, nor is he plotting to "show them" that he is not a failure. Will needs to become thin for himself, not to prove others wrong.

10. **Be grateful, humble, and generous with all you receive.** The process of manifesting and receiving is ongoing. Just as cleaning the vessel is an ongoing process, so is examining your motives, removing any static, and uncluttering yourself. Will needs to understand that he will be engaged in an ongoing process en route to finding his thin body, and he may also discover his core issues related to the central issue in his life. Whenever you manifest your intentions, you want to be grateful for the privilege of personal power. There is a tendency to brag, boast, or to be egotistical about your results. This attitude will only drive the blessings away. The right attitude to have when your intention lines up with the reality of the situation is an attitude of gratitude. Being humble, rather than arrogant, acknowledges the role of a higher power working on your behalf. Generosity, rather than greed, recognizes that none of

us ever does anything alone. Sharing the goodness allows others to experience their contribution to the outcome of the situation. The combination of gratitude, humility, and generosity equals the friendly environment that encourages future manifestations to appear.

FOCUS ON AN OBJECTIVE

In alignment with the laws of manifestation, coaching always focuses on a specific objective. Having an objective is one of the differentiating factors that separate coaching from consulting, therapy, and casual conversations. When the coachee has an objective, it creates a definite focus. Something is valued, and since it is, the coachee is willing to invest time, energy, and money to cause a shift in perspective and consequently formulate a request of the universe and of the self. It means he or she is willing to embark on the journey, from problem to solution. Objectives act as a rudder and provide direction so that the coaching session doesn't deviate from its purpose or become distracted with ancillary concerns. When coachees formulate their objectives, they initiate a process. The process involves coachees thinking beyond the conditions that currently exist in their lives. Most people accept what *is* rather than challenging the status quo and asking, "What is *possible*?" The process of identifying an objective begins with engaging imagination. Imagination accesses your ability to form images, ideas, and connections to that which you have never previously considered. When you start to imagine the world of possibilities, beyond your present situation, you open up the magical door to your preferred future.

Anatomy of the "I Want" Moment

Consider the anatomy of desire, or the "I want" moment. When someone makes the shift from accepting what is, to considering what could be, several things happen. The first thing that occurs is that the coachee

opens up to five possibilities: (1) things could be different, (2) alternatives might be available, (3) there is the potential that the coachee could
do something about this situation, (4) the coachee might deserve to have
what he or she wants, and (5) the coachee might be willing to invest the
time, energy, effort, and resources required because the outcome of situation, and the coachee, are worth it.

Let's revisit Will, the overweight person. He looks in the mirror and
says, "I'm fat." If he accepts the status quo, then he engages in mental conversations that excuse, explain, and justify why this is so. "I am big-boned.
I have a sweet tooth. I have no self-control. Everyone in my family is large.
I like to enjoy life. I have a slow metabolism. Everyone in my family has
thyroid issues; thyroid issues have permeated our family for generations."
If the overweight person has reconciled himself to being fat, then he has
either accepted his fate or given up on the possibility that things could
ever be different, or both. "I am fat, and that is that!" The entire issue
becomes a closed matter.

If, however, Will looks in the mirror and says, "I'm fat," and his next
thought is, "I want to be thinner than I am," then he has, in fact, launched
the process. He may be dissatisfied, angry, or just fed up with having the
same old issue, month after month, year after year. Whatever shifts his
frame of mind when he says "I want" is the significant factor that can
change his life forever. The "I want" moment is so powerful because it
presupposes that you have the right to desire something, that you possess
the self-esteem to change your reality, and that you contain the personal
efficacy to permanently alter your circumstances. It is the moment when
you think beyond "things are the way they are" and shift to the notion
that "things can be different." This is the moment of motivation and
choice. This is not to say that there won't be a reversal, a setback, or an
impediment, but the initial activation of desire and choice has occurred.

The Steps in the Coaching Process

When coachees imagine something different from what currently exists, they begin to build a bridge to their desired future. They start to believe things could be different than they are presently, they feel capable of articulating their wishes, and they feel worthy to have *something* the way they want it. Articulating an objective presumes that the coachee dares to consider having what he wants. In addition, he is bold enough to communicate that wish to another person and risk rejection, invalidation, and criticism.

Articulating a clear objective is the first step in the process of getting what you want. The second step is believing that what you want is possible. The third step is believing that *you* deserve to have what you want. The fourth step is embarking on a plan to build the bridge to your future, and the fifth step is soliciting support to get there, that is, asking a coach for help. The sixth step is getting reinforcement when you slide into confusion, doubt, uncertainty, and/or fear, and being reenlisted in your choice. Here again the coach possesses the objectivity to get the coachee back on track without negative judgments.

Articulating a clear objective. The coach helps build the bridge between here and there. You must first establish the "there" before you construct the bridge. The questions we ask to solicit objectives are: What in your life do you want to be different? What would you like to expand, enhance, or augment? What would you like to improve? Simple open-ended questions like these will encourage the coachee to volunteer an objective. Sometimes coachees don't know what they want. They might, however, know what they don't want. With a bit of probing, the coach can assist coachees in articulating what they want. This requires support, patience, and encouragement.

Believing that the objective is possible. The degree of negaholism that a person possesses will indicate the amount of belief in the objective that currently exists. If there is a considerable amount of doubt in the coachee's mind, the debate about the feasibility of the desire will engage.

Believing that the objective is deserved. Believing in the possibility of positive change and in your own capability are two different levels of belief. If coachees are going to make something happen, they must find their own intrinsic belief in themselves. Will had to believe in his own ability. He had to believe that his "desire" to find his thin body was possible. He had to make a leap of faith and overcome all of his fears, hidden decisions, beliefs, and considerations, and find the inner resources to believe in himself. Will found the desire, the willingness, the belief, and the commitment with the aid of his coach, who supported him in becoming his lean body.

Embarking on a plan to build the bridge. A plan marks the stepping-stones between the beginning point and the end point. The plan tracks progress and provides structure to measure results. In order for Will to believe his plan might work, he had to look at past successes, acknowledge his effectiveness in other areas of his life, and build a case for himself in order to restore faith in his abilities because he had eclipsed his successes with his defeats. His assignment was to examine his past and recall times when he had succeeded. He led the debate team to many victories, he was a gifted computer programmer, and he had a history of successful investing. Listing his successes helped him recall his accomplishments and start believing in his capabilities. In addition, he had to lay out all the steps that would eventually get him what he wanted.

Soliciting support in getting there. Rarely does anyone do anything alone. People are often the resource that cause things to happen. Asking others for support is yet another statement of belief in the project and in yourself. The next step in the process for Will was to determine who was supportive of his choice. He made a list that included his wife, his children, and a few close friends in whom he could safely confide. Additionally, he had to look at the people in his life who might disagree, disuade, or doubt him. He made a list of those as well. The first list showed Will who would be rooting for him. The other list included those who had seen him try over and over again and fail. They had lost their belief in his ability to become thin. He felt as if the two different groups were pulling him in two opposite directions. He realized that he needed to make this choice for himself and stop trying to please others or proving that he was able to do it.

Getting reinforcement. Reinforcement, encouragement, and support are necessary when there are setbacks or obstacles or when things look hopeless. In every mission that is worth envisioning and creating, there are often moments of doubt. Will would encounter many temptations. He would be strong at times, and at other times he would succumb. Part of the coach's job is to support him in getting back on track without beating himself up. Will would experience successes, and then he would slide backward. The coach would reinforce what he was doing right, and encourage him to keep on going. Just like an athletic coach will reinforce, recognize, and reward the young athlete, the life coach has the same role on the life journey.

STATED OBJECTIVES FOR COACHING

As we discussed earlier, clients have various reasons to be coached. Some of them are:

- To formulate goals and objectives
- To strategize lifelong dreams
- To resolve old issues
- To clear up communication breakdowns or blocks
- To solve problems
- To get perspective on a specific situation
- To have a sounding board
- To have a safe space (especially for high-profile people)
- To get "unstuck" from old behavior patterns
- To expand to the next level in their lives
- To break through an old issue
- To find a new direction
- To find a new profession

Formulating a Clear Objective

An objective is a specific item stated in the infinitive that:

- Has a quantifiable outcome
- Can be stated in one sentence
- Is agreed upon by both people
- Lends itself to an action plan
- Is achievable and actionable in the time frame allotted

Examples of workable objectives are:

- To increase my effectiveness at work
- To manage my time better
- To improve my relationship with my daughter
- To plan my year
- To organize the writing of my paper
- To improve my golf game
- To find time for things I love to do
- To find my thin body
- To start to live a smoke-free life
- To have beautiful hands (no more nail biting)
- To learn to use a computer
- To learn a new language
- To formulate a new self-image
- To live my life in trust and believe in myself (eliminate beat-ups)

Challenging Objectives

The objectives on the following list are a bit daunting for a new coach because they are too broad, too vague, or too abstract. Read them over and see if you can get your arms around them. They are:

- To stop being negative forever
- To be married
- To lose weight

- To improve my earnings
- To get control of my emotions
- To be more accommodating to co-workers
- To feel better
- To stop old patterns
- To stop addictions
- To be happier
- To stop worrying

An objective is a stated outcome. If the stated outcome isn't clear, you won't know when you have reached the destination. In addition, you want to state an objective in the positive, whenever possible. As we stated regarding Will, most people have a negative association with "losing" something. Losing your keys, your wallet, your umbrella, your sunglasses are all negative connotations. Then we take the same negative word and apply it to "losing weight" and wonder why people aren't enthusiastic. Rather than say, "I want to lose ten pounds," you might want to say instead, "I want to allow my thin body to be visible." It may sound silly, but it will stop automatic behavior and encourage conscious word choice. Rather than saying, "I want to stop smoking," something which you may enjoy, you might want to say, "I want to support my lungs and my overall health by living smoke-free." The words we use are important because they send a message to the brain that has either a positive or a negative association. When changing behaviors, minimize the discomfort, loss, and pain, and maximize the joy, positive outcome, and the benefit to you.

Objectives are difficult when they are:

- Too long
- Confusing
- Abstract, not concrete
- Too large to manage in the time allotted
- Vague, non-specific

• Lacking a clearly stated outcome
• Not stated clearly, articulately, or comprehensively
• Unwinnable

In a coaching session, Lucile stated her objective as: "I want to stop stressing." Her coach accepted her objective even though she felt uncomfortable with its lack of specificity and started asking questions. Lucile described all of the things that "stressed" her. She mentioned that, in fact, she was stressed most of the time. Being in a stressed-out condition was almost a way of life for her. Her coach dutifully followed her everywhere she went in her inventory of all the things that brought her stress. Eventually, the core of the issue emerged. Lucile was overly concerned about her family, and that was the cause of the majority of her stress. It took a lot of patience and a fair amount of time to complete the session; however, the coach never articulated the objective so both parties could hear and agree to it. If the coach had asked her from the beginning about the essence of her worries, they would have had a clear objective. In doing so, the session issue would have been resolved earlier. The objective needs to be articulated so that both coach and coachee engage in a verbal contract as close to the beginning of the session as possible.

MANIFESTING REALITY

Having an objective is being aligned with the law of attraction and manifesting. In order to manifest something, you have to be willing to state what you want. The universe cannot support, "I don't know." Imagine that there is a great restaurant in the sky. You sit down and the waiter approaches you. He asks, "What would you like?" You look at him and reply, "Something to eat." He probes further, "What would you like to eat?" and you reply, "Just bring me something from the kitchen." Since he isn't telepathic, he goes to the kitchen and brings Brussels sprouts. You look at him and say, "I don't like Brussels sprouts. Bring me something else." When the waiter returns, he shows up with marzipan cheesecake. You say, "But I don't like marzipan." He asks again, "What do you want?" At this point you have a choice: you can either get the message and ask for what you want, or you can keep doing what you're doing and expect different results. (By the way, that has been labeled the definition of insanity!)

When you ask for what you want, and you are willing to state it clearly and specifically, it presumes that you not only know what you want, but you also deserve to receive it. Stating what you want is the first bold and brave step to receiving what you want. In the process of formulating your request, you check in with yourself to determine what would please you at this moment in your life. Then you assess if your request is in alignment with the capability of the giver. For instance, you wouldn't request a hamburger in a vegetarian restaurant. The next step is to determine if you are up to the challenge of receiving what you have requested. For instance, if you requested a five-course prime rib dinner and you don't have the appetite, you might reconsider. Let's imagine that the giver is very generous and offers you a year of free dining wherever you choose. Your reaction might be disbelief, questioning what is expected in return, or asking, "Why me?" If the offer was legitimate, you might question your worthiness for such a generous gift. Consider asking for bigger and bigger requests. At some point, a little voice inside says, "That's enough!" or it may say, "That's too much!" The internal governor is powered by your self-esteem and always knows the appropriate request for you at each stage of your development. The key elements to manifesting your reality cannot be manipulated; they must emanate sincerely from your heart if they are to be realized.

Judith, an American living in Paris, had looked at more than thirty apartments to buy. This process had continued for over two years. She finally admitted that she was stuck. She commissioned a coach to work with her on the elusive home, who asked probing questions on what might be subconsciously going on with Judith regarding the apartment.

Judith finally realized that she felt uncertain and scared regarding all of the challenges of buying a home in a foreign country on her own. Fed up with her situation, she asked her coach to help her determine if it would be better for her to rent or to buy. They determined that more research was required on the international tax situation to assess the cost-benefit analysis. Judith's bookkeeper completed the research, which indicated that for the time frame that Judith wanted to own the property, it would make no difference financially if she bought or rented. When Judith discovered these results, she immediately began sending out e-mails for prospective apartments to rent. Her intention was to find an acceptable apartment in the area of Paris that she wanted, for the price she wanted, with all the specifications she had listed, within one week. She embarked on the mission, saw twelve apartments, and made her choice by the end of the week. She had lined up her options to make a choice, then committed to make it happen. She gave thanks for her coach, who helped her get unstuck, for her own willingness to do what it took, and for the manifestation of her intention.

⚜

In order to manifest your dreams, you have to be willing to state what you want. A statement of desire means that you are ready, willing, and able for change to happen. Embracing the future and letting go of the past enables you to move forward in your life. Coaching and change start with a clear objective. It isn't enough to follow the steps to manifesting the life you desire; you have to also examine your underlying motives, decisions, and beliefs. You may possess the motivation, perseverance, and commitment to keep on going regardless of the obstacles you encounter; however, for the person who would tend to give up when thwarted, a coach is a viable support to reaching the goal. A coach can help you deal with the challenges you encounter. Coaching is managed change.

Energy, Power Centers,
Chakras, and Flow

"Mystery creates wonder, and wonder is the basis
of man's desire to understand."
Neil Armstrong

Everything is energy. In the material world in which we live, it may be challenging to "see" energy; however, if you are sensitive you can definitely "feel" it. There is nothing in the world that is not composed of energy. In every conversation, there is an exchange of energy. Whether you are aware of it or not, energy is a key component of every interaction, and this is especially true in coaching sessions. In previous centuries, clocks with pendulums were the norm. If you put several clocks with pendulums in the same room together, the ticking of the clocks happened at different intervals. However, after several days in the same room, they would fall into a synchronous pattern. This is not a coincidence but rather a law of physics that states that vibratory frequencies in a closed system or room will reach the most stable, lowest energy state. The pendulums in the clocks become entrained.

Humans also have a vibration or electrical pattern that is constantly emitted. When people gather in a closed system or room with each other, their energy also will begin to oscillate at the same frequency. The heart is to the human what the pendulum is to the clock. Whether we are discussing clocks or humans, when they are placed in the same space together, eventually they will all oscillate to the same frequency. In coaching, when two people are focused on one concern, the energy of two—two hearts, two heads, two spirits aligned and intending for the right solution to surface—creates magical results. When we address the energy in a coaching session, we must include the seven chakras.

CHAKRAS

Chakras are energy centers. *Chakra* is a Sanskrit word meaning wheel of energy, or vortex, and it refers to each of the seven consciousness centers that transform energy and interface between the dense physical world of the five senses and the subtle world of pure consciousness. Chakras, or energy centers, function as pumps or valves, regulating the flow of energy through our energy system. Chakras each have a unique purpose. They can connect a specific part of you with another part of a person and can enable you to send a specific type of energy. The main chakras are located along the central meridian of your body, starting at the base of your spine and culminating at the top of your head. The functioning of the chakras reflects choices and decisions we make concerning how we respond to conditions in our lives. We open and close these valves when we decide what to think, what to feel, and through which perceptual filter we choose to experience the world around us.

The chakras are a concentrated part of the nonphysical body or aura. They are much less dense than the physical body. Chakras interact with the physical body through two main vehicles: the endocrine system and the nervous system. Each of the seven chakras is associated with one of the seven endocrine glands and also with a group of nerves called a *plexus*. Therefore, each chakra is associated with a particular body part and function. When chakras are vibrating with strong and clear energy, they effectively support the health and vitality of the corresponding areas of the body.

Neil, an accountant at one of the top accounting firms in Holland, had pain in his abdomen. He is talented with numbers; however, his passion is to play and write music. He believes that he can't make a living with his music and keeps it as his hobby. It is not surprising that Neil's pain is located in his power chakra since he experiences a lack of power to cause his dream to happen.

When you feel tension in your body, you also experience it in the chakra associated with that part of your consciousness. *Where* you feel stress depends on *why* you feel the stress. The tension in the chakra is detected by the nerves of the plexus associated with that chakra, then transmitted to the parts of the body controlled by that plexus. When the tension continues over a period of time, or to a particular level of intensity, the person creates a symptom on the physical level.

Margaret was having a difficult time saying "no." She had recently taken an executive position that prevented her from caring for her family. Not wanting to disappoint anyone, she would say "yes" when she really felt "no." Tasks that were not a choice for her were becoming an issue. When she got acute laryngitis, she was dismayed. She had no idea that what appeared to be a simple issue could have physical consequences. She had to take time off to heal her throat and look deeper at the "coincidences" in her life and what they were trying to say to her. It is no accident that Margaret's symptom is located in her fifth chakra because it is related to communication.

The symptom speaks a language that suggests that physical symptoms have lessons to teach us, and the metaphoric significance of the symptom becomes apparent when the symptom is described from the point of view of lesson rather than fate. Thus, rather than saying, "I can't see," we can describe it as keeping ourselves from seeing something. "I can't walk" means we have been keeping ourselves from walking away from a situation in which we are unhappy. And so on.

The symptom serves to communicate to us through our bodies what we have been doing to ourselves in our consciousness. When we change something about our way of being, in effect, "getting" the message or lesson communicated by the symptom, the symptom has no more need to exist, and so it can be released, according to whatever we allow ourselves to believe or imagine is possible. This notion is not be used against yourself in your present condition.

Understanding the chakras allows you to understand the relationship between your consciousness and your body, and then to see your body as a road map of your consciousness. It also gives you a better understanding of yourself and those around you.

You are in the process of opening up and taking control of your power. Chakras are power centers. Each chakra has a different function or purpose. When you become aware of your chakras and the power they have for you, you will have increased ability and control over your life force and will be able to use your energy in a deliberately constructive and empowering manner. Awareness of your energy centers will enable you to develop a rheostat for each one of your chakras, which means that you will be able to open and close each chakra at will. Let's address each chakra, and consider its function and purpose.

The first chakra, the "root" chakra, is located at the base of the spine. The root chakra's energy is about grounding, security, survival, and primal energy. The associated color is red, which corresponds to the musical note C; it relates to the Earth element, governs all elimination, the survival instinct, and the emotion of fear. When you become afraid of not being able to pay your bills, of a disaster happening to your child, or of a world war, you are operating from your first chakra.

The second chakra, the "sacral" chakra, is located below the navel, and its energy is about sexuality, creativity, and reproduction. The color is orange, which corresponds to the musical note D; it relates to the water element, governs the sex drive, the urogenital system, and the emotion of desire. When you are designing a presentation, being aroused by your partner, or become pregnant, you are operating from the second chakra.

The third chakra, the "navel" chakra, is located in the solar plexus, and its energy is about inner strength, will, "gut feelings," vitality, self-control, and power. The color is yellow, related to the element of fire, which corresponds to the musical note E; it governs the digestive system, the ego impulse, and the emotion of anger. When you have suppressed anger, a gut feeling, or you feel very powerful or powerless, you are operating from your third chakra.

The fourth chakra, the "heart" chakra, is located in the middle of the chest, and its energy is about love, compassion, forgiveness, and self-esteem. The color is green, which corresponds to the musical note F; it relates to the air element, the circulatory system, the individualized soul, and the emotion of love. When you forgive a friend, feel compassion for one less fortunate than you, or feel love for yourself or another, you are operating from your fourth chakra.

The fifth chakra, the "throat" chakra, is located in the neck, and its energy is about communication, healing, speech, and expression. The color is blue, which corresponds to the musical note G; it relates to ether, the respiratory system, the power of communication within yourself and with others. When you are involved in communicating, have laryngitis, or experience writer's block, you are operating from your fifth chakra.

The sixth chakra, the "third eye," is located between the eyebrows, and its energy is about intuition, insight, psychic awareness, and clairvoyance. The color is indigo, which corresponds to the musical note A; it relates to the mind, the individual self, the power of inner perception, and insight beyond the five senses. When you have precognitive dreams, when you know what is going on with your loved one, or when you have deep insights about yourself or others, you are operating from your sixth chakra.

The seventh chakra, the "crown" chakra, is located at the top of the head, and its energy is about higher consciousness, enlightenment, inspiration, and spirituality. The colors are white and violet, which correspond to the universal self, divine reality, and the power of consciousness. The crown chakra's musical note is B. When you feel connected to a higher source, become inspired to do something, or write with fluidity, it means that you are operating from your seventh chakra.

One of the simplest ways to support chakra energy is to visualize a flowing beam of white light coming down from high above you, into the crown of your head, all the way down through your entire body, and out your feet. You can breathe in deep, cleansing breaths with this visualization, and imagine any negative energy releasing easily out your feet. Supporting the vitality and flow of your own chakras helps you prevent yourself from absorbing any negative energy from a coaching session. Your coachees are also supported, because as your chakras and energy field are clear and strong, they act as catalysts, helping your coachees in more easily aligning their own chakras and energy field.

In every coaching session, you want to have your chakras open, aligned, and available. Having said this, you need to be extremely aware and careful of your second and sixth chakras' energies. The reason for this is that the second chakra flows sexual energy in both directions and is obviously inappropriate in a session. In a coaching session, you become connected and intimate with your coachee. It is extremely important to maintain this intimacy in a pure, nonsexual mode rather than crossing the line from professional coach to sexual partner. This would not only be unethical, it would also be a misuse of your power. You never want to cross this line with your coachees. Therefore, a heightened awareness of your sexuality and any sexual energy emanating from your second chakra is essential to being an outstanding transformational coach.

The sixth chakra is related to knowing and seeing. Since the purpose of the coaching session is to draw the inner truth (or spiritual DNA) from the coachee, this energy is also inappropriate in this type of session. If you keep your third eye open, you will receive information that will shift your energy into the "knowing" position. If you have your third eye open and active, you will not be empowering coachees in discovering their own answers; instead you will be "seeing" their answers, and that information will inhibit their discovery process. Conversely, if your third eye is not active, you will still be using your intuition, but it will come to you in the form of questions rather than in the form of answers. A hunch, gut feeling, or "message" is different from knowing what is going on with the other person. Therefore, you will need to disconnect from the sexual energy of your second chakra and the clairvoyance (clear seeing or spiritual vision) of your sixth chakra. However, continue to access the creativity of your second chakra and the intuition of your sixth chakra to support coachees in discovering their own truth. If you have previously been unaware of your chakras, then this fine-tuning will require considerable practice.

The most powerful chakras in a coaching session are the third, fourth, fifth, and seventh. The third chakra is your power chakra and is important to transmit power to your clients to empower them through their own doubts and fears. The fourth chakra is critical in creating a safe environment for your clients, as well as your pure heart connection. The fifth chakra supports clear communication. The seventh chakra is your connection with spirit, and enables you to receive inspiration and higher consciousness. When you ground yourself, combine power, heart, communication, and spirituality, you have the perfect combination for connection, safety, communication, and empowerment.

Knowledge of chakras coupled with regular use in your sessions will enhance your coaching. Heightened awareness, alignment, and the intentional use of your energy to empower another will make your coaching extremely connected and powerful.

Flow

Flow is the steady, unbroken, and continuous stream of energy between two or more people. It is also the psychological and physical experience that results in heightened states of awareness, confidence, and performance. When you are in the flow, the energy moves easily without constraint. Flow is about connection and alignment with the universal source of energy. Flow is without effort, struggle, or force. Flow is mindless and is our natural state; however, because of stress, so much of our lives are out of flow. Let's examine what impedes or blocks flow in a coaching session.

Thinking

When I say *thinking*, I mean the cognitive activity in your brain that starts chattering at you. Examples of thinking that impede the flow in coaching are: "Was that the right question to ask? She looks uncomfortable . . . should I say something to her? Her eyes look moist . . . maybe I should find some tissue. I'm lost; what question should I ask?"

When you start to think about what you should or shouldn't be doing, you break the flow of energy. That doesn't mean that it cannot be repaired; however, if you are to return to flow, you must be conscious and focus on mending the tear in connection in order to get back on track. Telling the truth is the most effective way to get back in flow. For example: "I'm confused. Can you clarify what you mean by . . . ?"

Trying to Figure Out the Answers

When coachees relate their situations to you, you listen intently to their words, you are in flow, and as a result, you "hold" the space for your coachees to be able to discover their own answers. When you go into your head, you break the flow because you try to figure out their situation for them. When you do this, you are saying with your behavior that you don't trust that they can and will derive their own answers, that they are capable of solving their own challenges, but rather that you are more capable than they of solving their problems. Going into your head definitely breaks the flow. In order to reestablish the connection, you need to notice it, refocus your energy, and reconnect with the coachee.

Judging the Coachee

A coachee may say something that triggers a judgment during a session. For instance, Julie was being coached on her marriage. She was trying to determine if she wanted to stay in her marriage or leave her husband. The situation isn't as simple as Julie would like it to be. She loves her husband, Jake, but she isn't *in* love with him. Jake provides for Julie and their two children; however, Julie has a shroud of sadness that hangs over her shoulders. She doesn't really want to leave, but she isn't happy staying in her relationship either. She is in limbo, and she spends a significant amount of time thinking about her situation each day. To stay or to leave is what continually occupies her thoughts. In the middle of their session, Julie's coach started to judge her. The coach thought, *You have it really great. Jake is a great guy, and he is really good to you. Most women would envy you and would do anything to have a husband like Jake. You are spoiled and should be happy with your situation. I can't believe that you are complaining.*

Judgments like these break the connection between Julie and her coach. Not only do the judgments take the coach out of present time, but they also create energetic separation. Judgments always create distance between you and your coachee. To return to flow, notice the judgment, write it on your pad, set it aside, resume suspended judgment, and continue with the session in a clean, unbiased state.

Being Out of Present Time

Many elements can take you out of present time. Distractions, mind chatter, thinking about the tasks you need to do, concerns about people, finances, and time constraints are among some of the top items. When your attention deviates from the coachee, you break the flow of the session. In a coaching session, you want to be there 100 percent for your coachee. You want to eliminate any and all clutter from your mind so that you are totally present for the precious moments that you are together. Thoughts like, *I have to pick up lettuce on the way home; I must mail that package to Lori; I need to call Julio about my printer,* will snatch you right out of present time and break the flow with your coachee. In order to get back on track, you want to notice the thoughts, jot them down, refocus, and reextend your energy so that the flow reengages.

Fear

Coaching sessions happen in the energy of trust. You trust coachees to find their own answers; you trust yourself to hold the space for them to discover their truth; you trust the universe to honor this moment and respond to the request for answers. Fear breaks the flow of a session. When you become afraid in a session, your energy field contracts, your breathing becomes shallow, and your blood vessels constrict. Fear impedes the flow of energy in your own body, and it also inhibits the flow between two people. When your thoughts move toward fear, you cannot trust because fear and trust are antithetical. If you are trusting, you are unafraid and vice versa.

Ideally, if you are fearful of something, you will be aware of it prior to the session and set those fears aside on a piece of paper or in a session that you have with your own coach. If you are unaware of your fears, the chances are that the coachee might mirror them back to you and trigger them coming to the surface. For instance, if you have financial fears, and your coachee begins to talk about the huge project that she is launching, and she states, "I am just afraid of the scope of the project and the amount of funds I need to generate," those words could easily trigger your own concerns and fears about finances, if you hadn't already addressed them. Deal with your fears whenever possible before you sit down with a coachee, then you will be centered and won't be caught off guard. If you notice that your own fears are triggered in a session, note it on your pad, make a mental note to revisit this later, and then reconnect with your energy to empower your coachee.

Trying to Do It Right

Coaching happens when you are connected and aligned with yourself. Being in flow means that you are listening and trusting that the connection, the transmission of energy, and the exchange of information is happening just the way it is supposed to. When you become intimidated by the person you are coaching, you can easily shift into trying to do the session "right." When you do this, you break the flow of energy because you are no longer at one with yourself, but are "efforting" at doing the session correctly so that it impresses the coachee. If you notice that someone intimidates you, see if you can equalize the relationship. This doesn't mean that you must diminish the coachee, or inflate yourself, but rather see both of you as humans doing your individual parts in the grand scheme of things. This may take some practice, as you might initially perceive some people as better or worse than you. The goal is to see each person as the unique individual he or she is, not better or worse, just different and special in their own unique ways.

Being Right

A coaching session is not about being right or wrong. If you become invested in being "right" in a session, you will break the flow. You will become engaged in a competitive quest for proving that you are right. When one person is right, the other is wrong. If your coachees feel "wrong," the energy is not conducive to supporting them in their wishes or goals. As a coach, you must give up any need to be right in the context of a session. You must engage in win-win interactions that empower your coachee. If you find yourself striving to be right, notice it, let it go, reconnect with your coachee, and get back into flow.

In a session, Bill used the word *preventative*. His coachee said, "The word is *preventive*." They started to argue about whether the word is *preventative* or *preventive*. Each person believed he was right, and the energy shifted to a power struggle of right versus wrong. This is not the best energy for a coaching session. Being right is not worth sacrificing the flow of energy. Let your coachees be right, even if you know they are not. As it turned out, the dictionary states that both forms are acceptable. They were both right. This was an unnecessary waste of connectivity and flow.

Worry

A coaching session will at some point focus on the coachee's ideal outcome or situation. In every session there will be a question addressing vision or fantasy. It is antithetical to the energy of the session for you to worry during the session. You could worry about whether the coachee will get what he or she wants, whether the coachee thinks you are a great coach, whether you are asking the right questions, whether the coachee's vision is realistic or not. You could worry about what the coachee is thinking, feeling, or imagining. You could worry about almost anything; however, it is not in your best interest or the coachee's to worry.

Set aside all of your concerns and worries for the duration of the session. Focus your attention on the coachee, and get the attention off of yourself. Ask questions regarding what the coachee is feeling, what the coachee is thinking, what the coachee wants, and stay connected while gathering important information. If you are worried about what the coachee thinks of you, you are probably caught in the approval syndrome. You need to address the approval syndrome when you notice it before your next session.

The Approval Syndrome

The approval syndrome is a system based on outer-centered reality that reinforces and feeds on itself. There are several beliefs that build on each other and form the syndrome. They are:

- I am not okay the way I am (the initial decision).
- I must seek agreement from others to prove that I am okay, and therefore a lovable and desirable person.
- I must do what others expect me to do, and ensure my behavior is acceptable and appropriate so that I won't risk losing their approval.
- I must always check with others to see what they expect, and align with their expectations and standards of acceptability.
- I must never act without checking with others first for fear of losing my status, approval, acceptance, and love.
- I certainly don't know what is best for me.
- Others know better than I do what is best for me.
- I need others' advice in order to avoid making a mistake that would cause me to lose face in their eyes.
- I must do everything "right" in order to avoid making a mistake and subsequently lose others' approval, love, or acceptance.
- My acceptability rests in doing what I "should" do and what I am "expected" to do. I must never deviate from that course.
- I must never look within myself for fear that what I see or feel won't align with those whose approval I seek.

If you suffer from the approval syndrome, you have work to do. The approval syndrome is a mental construction of "outer-centered reality." Outer-centered reality means that your center is external to yourself and is located in others, whom you hold in higher esteem than you hold yourself. If you are to be a "brilliant" transformational coach, you need to reclaim your center. If you are coaching someone who is outer-centered, you need to gently see if they are willing to shift from making decisions to please others to making choices that are personally and spiritually fulfilling. This is initially an additional challenge. If the coachee is outer-centered, the best he or she will be able to do is to make a decision as opposed to a choice.

CREATING A "BRILLIANT" SESSION

In Chapter 2, we gave our checklist for a "brilliant" coaching session. A "brilliant" session is one in which you are fully present, in flow, and being your true, authentic self. A "brilliant" session dances with energy, combines heart, power, and spirit, incorporates the chakras, empowers through empathy, and supports the choice that the coachee is willing and wants to make.

A "brilliant" session happens when there is a beautiful and precious exchange of energy between two people. The coach, while maintaining control, is in service to the coachee and empowers the coachee to make his or her choice. When you do a "brilliant" session, it means that you are conscious of the energy, the flow between the two of you, and you manage expectations so that they are exceeded. It means that effortless energy illuminates the objective and provides resolution. It means that the mission is accomplished in an elegant and deeply connected manner.

❧

The focus and integration of feelings, energy awareness, creating and maintaining flow, the integration of the chakras, messages, the use of mirrors, the "wow factor", the brilliant session, processing issues, creating positive imprints, and living the process are the key elements that differentiate the MMS transformational coaching process from any other type of accountability coaching. With practice and awareness, your coaching will be truly transformational.

Living the Process

7

"Happiness is when what you think, what you say,
and what you do are in harmony."

Mahatma Gandhi

The difference between an average coach and a truly "brilliant" coach has everything to do with living the process. We can teach most people how to ask curious questions. We can teach participants in our program how to focus their attention, how to quiet the voices of the mind, and how to effectively use their energy. All of the core competencies of the MMS coaching method are ultimately not that difficult to learn. The most challenging part of training individuals in how to become extraordinary coaches is in living the principles that they are coaching. It is easy to mechanistically learn the tools, techniques, types of sessions, and forms; however, to embody the principles of coaching, as a living example, is ultimately what separates a good coach from a great one. Many coaches operate in the "do what I say, not what I do" model, but that doesn't equate to a transformational coach.

Truly empowering coaches are those who listen to their "messages," trust them, and are ready and willing to take action. They are committed to their own growth and development, take risks, and learn from everything that happens to them. They are willing and able to experience all of their feelings, to keep "the vessel" clean, and to live their lives with integrity. They are willing to see the mirrors in their sessions, in their lives, and they use them as opportunities to grow. They reach out when they are stuck, ask for support, and are open to receiving it. They model the coaching process in their lives and go for their dreams, visions, and goals. When they are at a plateau, have accomplished all of their goals, are ready for the next level, or find themselves challenged, they schedule sessions with their own coaches to see what they must do to go to the next level. They so believe in the coaching process that they can be looked to as not only leaders, but also as role models. You can tell if coaches are authentic by the way they look you in the eye. You can tell whether they walk their talk and if there are any inconsistencies between what they say and what they do. You can tell from the stories they share about their life process. If they are authentic, there is a ring of integrity that you can feel. The way in which coaches conduct their lives will provide you with clues as to the quality of people they are and in turn the quality of their coaching. You can also tell great coaches by interviewing their clients to see if their growth is mirroring their coaches' development. If they are great coaches, they should be continually moving and growing.

When coaches embrace the MMS coaching way of life, they are saying that they are committed to fulfilling their highest potential, and in turn are here on Earth to support others in doing the same. They are committed to fulfilling their life purpose rather than arguing for their limitations. They want to make their dreams and the dreams of others come true rather than having reasons, excuses, and explanations. There is a profound shift that happens when you live the coaching process. You actually change the way you live:

From ...	To ...
Living in the past and the future	Living in the present
Wishing and hoping	Attracting and manifesting
Having your life be about receiving acceptance, attention, recognition, and avoiding rejection	Having your purpose in life be to grow, learn lessons, and honor yourself and empower others
Figuring out how things should be	Trusting your process unconditionally
Judging your circumstances	Using your circumstance as an opportunity for growth
Fear, worry, and hope about the future	Trusting yourself, the process, and a higher power
Competing and getting "yours"	Serving and supporting others
Others will do it for you	You are at cause
Having to change or fix things	There is a perfection to the way things happen (even if we cannot see it at the time)
Life is real	Life is an illusion that can be designed the way you want it

If you're not getting what you want in your life, it is difficult to support others in getting what they want. For example, if you are not meeting your quotas at work, unconsciously you won't want to support colleagues in achieving or exceeding theirs. If you are unhappy in your relationship, you won't be inclined to support a friend in making his or her relationship magical. Instead, you might commiserate on why the opposite gender is so difficult and build a case using both of your examples as proof. If you aren't delighted with your home environment, you won't delight in shopping for your colleague's new apartment. If you are having trouble eliminating smoking from your life, it might seem hypocritical for you to support a relative in stopping the same habit. The "I can help you, but I can't help myself" attitude doesn't work in transformational coaching. You need to lead the way for others to follow, espousing, "If I can do it, then so can you!"

Conversely, if areas of your life are working, you naturally want to share the good news and blessings. If you are exceeding your quotas at work, you are willing to share your secrets of success because you are without any scarcity consciousness. If your relationship is harmonious and compatible, you want everyone you care about to be just as happy and fulfilled as you are. If your home is truly your castle, you will want others to feel the same rooted, cozy feeling when they are nestled at home. If you come from joy, abundance, and fulfillment, you want others to share in your happiness. The bottom line is that whatever your reality, you will want others to be a part of it, positive or negative.

Here is another of Lynn's personal stories:

I had been living in Holland for three years in a guesthouse, which was a quiet, cozy, and charming Amsterdam apartment. It had two floors, a garden outside the back window, and an entrance on an alley that was convenient for entering and exiting with ease. At the end of the third year, a series of events occurred that made the apartment less and less desirable. First, construction began on the buildings on both sides. Construction meant that noise became an issue. Drills, sledgehammers, and jackhammers filled the air from 7:00 AM until 6:00 PM. Since I also worked from my home office, sessions there were becoming inaudible. Second, the little alley that provided the entrance to my guesthouse was now enclosed with a temporary construction scaffold tunnel that made it dark, enclosed, and a dirt collector. Third, the construction started to envelope my sweet garden—what was once filled with sunlight, lush green trees, and birds was now dark, sunless, and surrounded with sheets of brown plywood blocking my view. Being a creature of familiarity and dreading the thought of uprooting myself and moving, it took me six months to confront the fact that I was miserable and had to move. Whenever someone would mention a new home or relocating, I would cringe, justifying the conditions with the thought that it was temporary. When I finally did make the choice to move, though, the thought of having a new, clean, and sunny apartment on the canal in the center of Amsterdam changed everything. And when I found my apartment, I felt so happy with my new circumstances that I was eager to help others find homes that made them as joyful as I was. Now that I feel rooted and grounded, I want others to feel that same delight.

Unless you first make peace with the person inside you and take care of your needs and wants, life can be a constant struggle. After all, *you* aren't going away—you'll spend the rest of your life with you. Others will come and go, but you'll always have you around, no matter what. If you aren't getting what you want, you could resent others getting what they want; it will be difficult to rejoice in their successes, especially when you look pitiable next to them. That doesn't mean that you need to compare, compete, or try to "keep up with the Joneses," but in order to honestly celebrate other people's successes, you want to ensure that you are happy and fulfilled within yourself at your level.

THE TWELVE STEPS TO LIVING THE PROCESS

These twelve steps sum up what it means to live the life of a "brilliant" transformational life coach, empowering others in manifesting their hearts' desires. To live the process is a bit like being the "fool" card in the tarot deck. You listen, trust, and do what your higher self indicates. You are willing to listen to your own inner wisdom and go where the messages, lessons, and guidance take you. When you live the process, you don't necessarily fit into the world of convention, but rather connect with your own purpose and align yourself with your value system and principles. When you live the process, you are committed to fulfillment rather than the trappings of success. You are dedicated to authenticity rather than position, prestige, or perks. You are devoted to the truth and honoring your ultimate purpose in life rather than momentary appetite gratification. It is because you have this unswerving allegiance to connection, meaning, and the deeper values in life that you have the ability to support your clients, colleagues, and friends in being loyal to their higher selves. When you live the process, you encourage, empower, and enkindle joy in others, aligning them with their true essence and values.

When Marie was a publicist in New York, she had worked her way up the corporate ladder from assistant to account executive. With a window office on Park Avenue, her own personal assistant, and a shining future in advertising and public relations, everything was hopeful and positive. She had been working in public relations for six years and had felt very proud of her accomplishments. When she visited San Francisco on a holiday, she had a deeply moving coaching session that changed her life. In addition to realizing that public relations was not her life's work, she discovered that her life's purpose was to be dedicated to empowering people through coaching. Additionally, she had the desire and the message to move to San Francisco, leaving her beloved New York, her prestigious, high-paying job, and the familiarity of her home city. She had to examine her priorities and determine what her next steps were. Within eight months, she moved across the United States, opened her own business in San Francisco, and rented out her New York apartment. The change process had officially begun, and she was on her way to creating her dream job in her dream city.

Read over the following twelve steps to living the process, and ask yourself if you are willing to live life from this joyful perspective. If you are, then you can truly live the life of a "brilliant" transformational coach.

1. **Enjoy every day of your life, and have fun doing whatever you do.** Enjoyment means to find the joy in whatever you are engaged in. Joy is not so much found in any particular action as it is created within the person who is performing the act. When you find the

joy within you, you bring it with you wherever you go, to whatever activity you do. It is part of you and dwells within you. When you are joyful, it is part of your essence and no one can take it from you.

Since Lynn moved into her new apartment, she says, "I have an overwhelming feeling of joy that flows into everything I do. Life seems lighter and more playful, and I have a feeling of ease with everything."

2. **Feel, experience, and honor your feelings.** Feelings are the outward expression of your innermost reality. Feelings enable you to connect with your authentic self. Emotions connect your physical self with your spiritual self and are a barometer of your overall well-being. Your feelings indicate how you are in relationship to yourself and others. When you allow your feelings, you show that you respect your reality. When you honor your feelings, you place your personal experience above saving face or pleasing others.

Claudia had difficulty finding her feelings and, conversely, when someone said or did something that touched her, she couldn't hold back the tears. When the tears began to flow, she could hardly shut them off and feared they would never stop. When the tears took over, she couldn't speak and was blocked in her throat chakra. Claudia discovered that she had an on/off switch with her feelings. She kept the switch off, and when someone flipped her switch to on, she lost all control of her emotions. What Claudia wanted was to be able to speak without crying, to find her voice, and to be more in charge of her feelings. In a coaching session, she discovered that when her father died, she had shut off the affective part of herself because the pain of his loss was too much for her to handle. She was nine years old at the time. For decades, Claudia managed her life through suppressing her feelings to figure out how to cope in each situation. The thought of opening up that closed door to her feelings was daunting to her. She realized that if she was to achieve her objectives, she had to finally mourn the death of her father.

There were, of course, other events in her life that she also had to mourn and release as well as that first loss, which was the root of her original decision to suppress her emotions. After she chose to mourn all of her losses, she could then express herself authentically without crying.

3. **Tell the truth, *your* truth, to the best of your ability.** Telling the truth means that you are connected to your essential self and your own perception of reality. It means that you look deeper than the surface explanation or your circumstances. Telling the truth means that you go beyond appropriateness and decorum, and reveal what is sometimes unspeakable. Telling the truth is about being your authentic self and letting others experience it, regardless of their reaction.

Claire's mother was an old friend of mine. She was concerned about her daughter's future and requested a session for her. Claire was very intelligent and had attended a top university, receiving a degree in architecture. She had also been a Web designer and had discovered that she didn't enjoy architecture or design. She was at a crossroads and didn't know what to do. I asked her many questions such as: What do you enjoy doing? What is fun for you? When do you feel most fulfilled? To every question that I asked, she replied, "I don't know." That isn't a very gratifying experience for a coach, but I continued. At one point I asked, "When was the last time you had a really good time?" She thought for a moment, and then a big smile came over her face. "It was a few months ago at my friend's apartment. She was having a party, and I was making the lasagna." She twinkled as she continued, "I had an apron on, and I had tomato sauce all over me. I loved working with my hands and making the layers of cheese, noodles, and sauce." I was amazed at her animation and enthusiasm, and I commented, "It sounds like you enjoy cooking." She looked at me with shock and said, "I love to cook!" I replied, "I'm a bit confused. You have been saying 'I don't know' repeatedly, but look at how you light up when I mention cooking. Am I missing something?" Her face lost its luster, and a scowl surfaced on her brow. "I could never be a chef, with all the money my mother spent on my education. She would kill me!" Telling the truth to yourself or a significant relationship isn't always easy, but it is important.

4. **Look within yourself for your messages, guidance, and direction . . . and when you discover it, trust it, honor it, and follow it.** Looking within means that you are devoted to the spiritual side of your nature. It means that you reflect on your options and choices before you act, checking in with your essence. Messages, guidance, and direction are always there if you are willing to take the time to listen and notice what they are indicating.

Daniel received a clear message about moving to Canada. He had reservations because it was far from home, colder than he preferred, and unfamiliar. Despite his apprehension, Daniel discussed the possibility with his boss and was subsequently reassigned to a position in Canada. He left family, friends, and the familiarity of all that he was accustomed to. He was prepared for the move; however, he was apprehensive about all the changes that he would experience. He felt that this was the right thing to do and believed that his trial year would let him experiment without having to make a lifetime commitment. After just three months, he believed he was in the right place, had made the right choice, and that this had been the perfect moment to launch into a new territory. He took the risk, trusted himself, and discovered new opportunities—and a whole new life opened up to him.

5. **Focus on solutions rather than on problems.** Your orientation to reality is to either dwell on the problem or on the solution. It is always your choice; however, the problem gives headaches and heartaches, while the solution provides a wonderful lightness of being. When you are committed to the solution, it means that you

won't allow the problem to slow you down, drag you down, or sour your spirit. It means that you always know there is a solution to every problem, and you strive to create win-win outcomes.

Nell constantly complained about her relationship. When asked how she was, she would start with, "Things are really hard with George." When asked, "What's going on?" she would start the litany of everything he did wrong, how he responded negatively, and how difficult it was to be in relationship with him. He was uncommunicative, distant, and inconsiderate. He didn't anticipate her needs, but thought only of himself. He was stingy and took more than he gave. He was sarcastic, diminishing, and derogatory. When asked, "Why do you stay with him?" she would always reply, "Because I love him!" She obsessed on the problems and could find very little positive to say. She was afraid of losing him, but she couldn't accept him as he was. For Nell to start living the process, she would need to focus on George's good qualities, why she chose him, and what was right about him. The alternative, if she couldn't focus on his blessings, was to exit the relationship.

6. **Believe in yourself, believe in others, and believe in the impossible.** Believing in yourself means that you hold yourself in high esteem. It means that you validate your accomplishments and celebrate your successes. It also means that you honor yourself and wouldn't consider demeaning or sabotaging yourself. You take time for your needs and wants, and you care for and about yourself. In addition, it means that you are willing to go for the "seemingly impossible," that which appears unreasonable to even want.

Johan was a big man who doubted himself at every turn. Through his utilization of the coaching process, he took each incident from his life that created self-doubt, looked it squarely in the eye, and healed it. It was a process that made him stand taller, breathe deeper, and speak with conviction. As a result of his methodical step-by-step process, he exuded self-reliance, self-trust, and self-confidence that were appropriate to a man of his stature.

7. **Be committed to moving in your life, reaching out for help, and/or having a coaching session when you get off track or "stuck."** This doesn't mean that you must be perfect, but rather that you are realizing many of your dreams and making definite strides toward the others. If you expect others to reach out to you, you must be willing to take personal inventory, notice when you are stuck, tell the truth, and do whatever you need to do to become unstuck. Living the process means that you are never too proud or too arrogant to reach out to other coaches to obtain support, encouragement, and validation. In other words, you practice what you preach, and you live what you teach.

Mimi was riddled with traces of negaholism from her family of origin. Despite the fact that she is bright, talented, and attractive, her nagging fear of the negative voices returning was ever present. When she discovered that she wasn't expected to be perfect, that she could reach out and have a coaching session if the voices ever returned, without embarrassment or chagrin, she felt relieved and peaceful. She could stop worrying about something that might never occur.

8. **Love yourself unconditionally, all the parts of you, and treasure who you are.** Conditional love means that you accept yourself only when you live up to the expectations and standards that you have established—when your body looks the way it should, when you produce the results that you have outlined, when you have the ideal relationship, and when your life is the perfect picture of success. When you love yourself unconditionally, you love and accept yourself when areas of your life are imperfect. When you are sick in bed, you still love yourself. When a big business deal has fallen through, you still love and accept yourself. When you have a fight with your best friend, you still love and accept yourself. When you let someone down, break an agreement, or unknowingly hurt someone,

you still love and accept yourself. This may sound like narcissism, but in actuality it is about treasuring who you are and honoring your relationship with yourself. When you don't live up to your standards, you look and see what the lessons are, learn them, let go, and move on.

Simone started out as a procrastinator who couldn't confront anyone. She didn't stand up for herself, she didn't initiate communication, nor did she believe that any positive change would happen if she did. She had issues with her boss, her clients, and her husband. As a result of her coaching sessions, Simone found the courage to initiate difficult conversations, to stand up for herself when she felt disrespected, and to completely eliminate procrastination. She started to embrace who she was, and she stopped giving herself any reason to ever beat herself up again.

9. **Pursue your dreams, your inspiration, your "higher self," and your messages.** Going for your dreams may not always be convenient. Life presents us with tests and lessons that beg the question, How much do you want it? When you go after your dreams, inspiration, and messages, you realize that you will be asked to stretch into larger shoes than you previously filled. If you are going to be an example to others, you need to show the way. Showing the way means leading others to their inspiration. When your path is filled with obstacles and you feel constantly thwarted when you attempt to book a flight, make the time to get your projects done, or inspire prospective clients to buy your product, then it is time to utilize your own coach to support you through those challenges and cause your desired results to happen.

Cassandra was engaged to Charles. Although she loved him, she continually doubted her choice. Through her coaching sessions, she started to get to the root of her doubt, which was based in her previous relationships with men. After she resolved each past relationship, including the relationships with both of her parents, she felt like a new woman. As a whole and integrated person, she could completely commit to Charles and believe in her heart that he was the perfect man for her.

10. **Reach out to a higher power when you need support.** You need to be willing to strive to see your circumstances from a higher perspective. You don't need to believe in a specific doctrine or religion, but you need to consider that higher powers are available to help when you are in need. Reaching out to a higher power, your angels, loved ones, or special souls who have crossed over means that you acknowledge your humanity, and you ask for help, guidance, or direction.

11. **Be responsible for your actions, and take charge of situations that you are able to resolve positively.** Being responsible doesn't mean that you are to blame. Being responsible means that you acknowledge that you are the cause in your circumstances. It means that you are willing to learn a lesson from everything that happens to you. It means that you are willing to take a leadership role in all areas that can possibly be resolved.

Harriet became more powerful as Robert, her husband, became more ineffective. When Harriet saw the pattern that she recreated from her mother, she admitted that she was reliving her family history. She wanted to change the future and not repeat the past. Unlike George and Nell, Harriet took a leadership role in reconciling their differences. She chose to take charge of the situation. She started to communicate her feelings and requests to Robert because most of the time he didn't think to ask. She also started to initiate conversations about their perceptions, beliefs, and expectations, which was also new to him. Robert wasn't used to conversations about topics that were deeper than weather, logistics, activities, sports, or current events. He was, however, willing to learn from Harriet, and as she led him, their relationship became stronger and more connected with each passing day.

12. **Regard everything in your life as a mirror, learn the lessons, search for the perfection in the grand scheme of things, and self-correct lovingly.** Your commitment to growth must be more important than your need to be perfect or to diminish yourself. You do not let pride nor stubbornness block you from seeing, discovering, and growing in every facet of your life. Seeing the perfection is not always easy. To see the perfection, you must have some perspective and an elevated viewpoint. When you see the perfection, you examine the situation from the point of view of being essential to teach you a lesson that otherwise you might not learn.

Irma saw that her negative self-concept was not only faulty, but it was keeping her from having positive relationships with her husband and three children. Like a hall of mirrors, her lack of enthusiasm was contagious, and the whole family started taking on her negativity. When she chose to change the behavior, the interactions among family members shifted. The change started with Irma recognizing her talents and then shining the light on the qualities of those around her. The whole game changed with one subtle commitment to positive self-recognition. One little change affected many people's lives.

If you are living the process, you are paving the way for all of your coachees who are interested in going for their dreams and making the seemingly impossible happen. In addition to living the process, you also want to stay in balance. Being in balance means that you know how to stabilize and care for your self.

BALANCE

If you are living in balance, you know your strengths and limitations. You know the amount that you can handle and the number of projects that will either create a condition of happiness or overwhelm you. You actively monitor your well-being on a daily basis. You can say "no" to yourself and others. You don't give in to temptation, but rather hold out for the long-term satisfaction of achieving your goals. Living in balance requires you to ask yourself some questions: If my life were in balance, what would that look like . . .

- At home?
- At work?
- At leisure?
- With family?
- With friends?
- Alone with myself?

In looking at balance and harmony, there are people who give you energy and others who take energy from you. Who are those people who drain you, and what can you do to release them from your life?

Frank was asked by the CEO of his organization to initiate a change project. That request meant taking over a department that included several colleagues with whom he used to work. They were now to become his direct reports. One of these colleagues, Ivan, was jealous of Frank accepting the position, and every time they interacted, Frank felt stressed and drained. After a coaching session, Frank realized that Ivan was not interested in his success. Frank also discovered that Ivan was not his first choice as a supporter in his new department. He had to inform Ivan that it wasn't going to work and that Ivan had to look for a new position. Although it was uncomfortable, Frank dramatically reduced the stress in his life from this one conversation. In addition to resolving issues at work, Frank's coaching session also revealed that he needed to modify his diet, eating better quality and smaller quantities of food, as well as needing to find some quiet time to be still each day. In getting to know himself, Frank found that he could manage the stress better and find homeostasis or balance.

When you live the process, you align who you are with what you do. You integrate all facets of yourself into one person who is led by the most positive and life-affirming part of you. When you live the process, you support others in living from their highest selves because you believe that is possible. When you live the process, people are drawn to you because of the light that you exude. When you live the process, you are honored to be able to serve others and bring more joy to the world.

Marketing and Building
Your Coaching Practice

"Just because something doesn't do
what you planned it to do doesn't mean it's useless.
Many of life's failures are people who did
not realize how close they were
to success when they gave up."

Thomas A. Edison

Once you have the spirit, the method, the desire, and the skills to be a "brilliant" coach, it is time to apply your knowledge and expertise to actively supporting people. You may be in one of five situations: (1) you work for a large corporation in which you will use your coaching skills in conjunction with your job description, (2) you create a situation with a firm that will actively refer clients to you, (3) you launch an independent coaching practice on your own, (4) you form an association with other coaches to complement each other's expertise, or (5) you use your coaching skills informally with family and friends. We'll examine each one of these.

Working for a Corporation as an Internal Coach

If you work for a corporation as an internal coach, you will either be directed to the individuals and groups whom you will be coaching, or you will propose targets, individuals and teams, whom you perceive will benefit from your skills and abilities. For instance, you might gain access to records that document underperforming teams or high-performance teams within the organization. You might then propose to improve productivity, monitor effectiveness, or create record-breaking results. Before you start the task, make sure you obtain baseline measurements so you can quantify your results. In addition, make sure you form a team of allies, on all levels of the organization, who will assist you in positioning yourself to make the maximum contribution, both to the organization and to the individuals who work there.

Jo-Anne Guderian is the managing broker for Coldwell Banker Premier Realty in the Centennial Hills office in Las Vegas. She took the MMS Coach Training. This is what one of her employees said:

I was in a state of indecision and had to make a choice about an important emotionally charged matter that involved my finances. After Jo-Anne asked me what the main issue was, she asked me a series of questions, and then repeated my answers back to me. It was interesting to hear my answers repeated. They sounded so different when they were not inside my own head! Jo-Anne continued with the process, addressing the questions and responses one by one. Suddenly, each concern became smaller as it was separated from the whole picture. The big picture became more manageable. Some concerns became insignificant and completely lost their power as we worked through the process. It became clear that part of my indecision was related to an absence of essential facts, so I discovered that I still had some work to do on my own. This was a relief, because it helped me to understand the reason I was stuck.

The decision was ultimately up to me, but the coaching helped me realize what I have gained from the entire experience of this choice, how to build myself back up from any disappointment, and how to carry on in a positive manner. I also learned that I could create a new dream every day, because our lives are always changing, and we have to adjust and be flexible. One cannot "force the issue" in circumstances that just don't make sense at that particular point in time.

Finally, we explored a new direction option, and where that would take me in five years. It was sensible, practical, and structured. I felt a burden lift from myself when we explored other possibilities. Since then, I have been open to new options and realized opportunities can disappear, but dreams cannot.

Jo-Anne uses her coaching skills to recruit new agents and to coach existing real estate agents on their sales and anything that might get in the way of them meeting their quotas. Jo-Anne said:

I am a manager of a real estate sales office, and I took the MMS Coach Training to increase my ability to work with and coach my agents to higher levels of success. However, what I gained has been much more than I imagined. The training has benefited me in both my marriage and my relationships with my children, which is invaluable, and, of course, in my relationship with myself! I recognize now when I am stuck on an issue and know when to reach out and ask for help, of course from a graduate of the training. In my work environment, I have discovered that I am able to connect with people at a deeper level in the coaching process and in deal-ing with people in general, be they sellers, buyers, or potential recruits. And I help my agents with much more than their real estate sales, helping them work through personal issues as well as career issues. What I know is that when people are happier in all areas of their lives, they are much more likely to succeed in their chosen profession; this is a true win-win outcome. The MMS Coach Training has definitely helped me with what was the daunting task of starting an office from scratch. It has eased the process, and I am very grateful for the opportunity to take the program.

Karen Daleboudt is a leadership development consultant (coaching and mentoring) at ABN AMRO Bank in the Netherlands. Using her skills from the MMS Coach Training, she helps business units of the bank establish coaching programs. Karen assists them in creating a framework for coaching and matches coaches with managers. She helps executives in setting their coaching objectives and creates the right matches between executives and external coaches.

Another team working effectively together is at Paragon Decision Technology, a software company with offices in the United States, the Netherlands, and Singapore. The three principals of Paragon took the MMS Coach Training together. Gijs Dullaert (president and CEO), Gertjan de Lange (vice president of sales and marketing), and Marcel Roelofs (chief technology officer) have teamed up to use their coaching skills both internally and externally—among themselves as a management team, with their staff, and with their customers.

Former KPN, the Dutch Telecom market leader, executive Herman Waijers has committed his coaching skills to change projects. He divides his time between being a management consultant and running his firm, TOP Business Partners, BV, currently consisting of fourteen associates. In both functions he constantly uses his coaching skills. Additionally, MMS coach Anke Waijers, Herman's wife, sometimes joins his companies' projects to bring additional quality to the team.

ARE YOU AN EMPLOYEE OR AN ENTREPRENEUR?

There is a significant difference between someone who works for a corporation and a person who starts his or her own company. If you work for a corporation, you have a job description, a salary, benefits, days and hours that you are expected to work, a vacation, a boss, and certain expectations that you must meet in order to keep your job. You have performance reviews, company activities, and a group of people with whom you must integrate.

If you are an entrepreneur, you have a clear sense of what you want. You may have a vision or even a dream, but you possess the enthusiasm, energy, inner direction, and capacity to operate in the void (without knowing where your next client will come from). You also have a willingness to do whatever is needed and wanted. The core differences between being an employee and being an entrepreneur have to do with structure, discipline, self-management, and the ability to handle uncertainty. One situation is not better than the other. Self-employment may look attractive because of the freedom, flexibility, opportunity, and limitless earning power. Having a job may seem enticing because of the predictable salary, clear expectations, limited responsibility, and the possibility to do a job without it consuming your life.

You must determine for yourself if you are an entrepreneur or an employee. No one can determine this for you. It ultimately comes down to whether you can function at optimum performance without the framework of a job. If the condition of flying by the seat of your pants makes you so uncomfortable that you are in a state of anxiety, then you should be working in a salaried position. If working in a job, for a boss, in a company makes you feel confined or claustrophobic, then you need to be your own boss. Only you can determine what is right for you; however, knowing what's true about you will save you a lot of consternation, worry, and wasted time. A coaching session will assist you in determining what type of person you are and is essential to saving you time and energy.

A Hybrid Solution

Jasmine, a human-resource professional at a prominent bank in Belgium, left the bank to set up her own coaching practice. When she communicated to her boss that she was going independent, he asked if the bank could be her first client. She set up her coaching practice with her first fifteen coachees referred from the bank. Since she knew the banking culture and the challenges her bank faced, she was the ideal choice.

This is an example of a "direct feed," a noncompetitive resource that actively sends you clients on a regular basis. When corporate employees go into business for themselves, they can often turn their corporate clients into clients for their own firm. For example, you may be an interior designer and have an affiliation with a real-estate agent. Every time the agent closes a sale, she refers her new client to you. People who trust this Realtor will take note and follow her lead. If you don't have a direct feed such as this, then you will need to market what you do in a strategic manner.

Launching an Independent Coaching Practice

If you decide to become an independent coach and build your own business, your first step is to ascertain your niche. You need to assess the experience, expertise, knowledge, and talents you have to offer to the marketplace.

For example, Alberto was an Italian who relocated to the Netherlands. After he became a Dutch citizen and completed the MMS Coach Training, he assessed his skills, abilities, experience, expertise, and passion. Alberto is fluent in many languages, including Dutch and, of course, his native language, Italian. He has moved to a foreign country, learned the culture, the traditions, the geography, and the people and has adjusted to a whole new life. He knows from the inside out the challenges an expatriate experiences, since he has personally had to navigate this labyrinth. Alberto deduced that because of his background, experiences, and expertise, he would use his coaching skills to help other "expats" adjust to living in the Netherlands. Alberto has conducted his market research, has identified his niche, and is launching his coaching practice. Just like Alberto, you can connect the dots in your life and determine the specific niche where you can contribute.

Maria also identified her niche. She was the managing director of her family business for fifteen years. An import-export business in Hong

Kong, the business under her guidance employed 135 people, eight of whom were family members spread over three generations and with all of the intricate relationship challenges working with family entails. As a result of her experience of running a multi-million Euro family business, she has chosen to launch a family business coaching practice and has taken her talents to a familiar market.

Teaming Up with Complementary Coaches

Another option is to form a team with several other coaches who have complementary yet different specialty areas. For example, one coach might be a specialist in interior design and join with another coach who specializes in architecture, another who is a general contractor, and a final member of the team who is in real estate. Complementary skills and specialties coupled with alignment in method make for a winning combination. Then when a new client pursues a goal in a related field, you can provide "one-stop shopping." When all the coaches use the same method, it allows for congruency, consistency, and smooth integration. Clients feel served, and the team can confer easily if necessary.

A unique five-member association in Holland has combined the talents of a human-resource manager/line manager, a multinational executive, a professor, a strategic consultant, and an executive-search professional. The team has formed a partnership to work together on projects in many diverse fields.

Informally Coaching Family and Friends

You can also use your coaching skills informally with family and friends. Informing those close to you that you are available for problem-solving, support for concerns, transitions, and offering a helping hand when you see it is needed, will open more doors. Some people like to offer their skills to loved ones or nonprofit groups without financial compensation, and others start with family members to become comfortable before venturing out into the business world. Regardless of how you utilize your newly developed skills set, you want to be actively choosing the application of your talents.

CULTIVATING REFERRALS

Your best source of new business comes from referrals from your current clients. Lynn is a master enroller of corporate coaching clients. She has a way of attracting business that is worthy of note. For example, she worked with a client, Larry, who ran the small business division of a major telecommunications company. This account was worth $25,000 a month in fees. One morning Larry called to let Lynn know that his job had been terminated. Not only had his job disappeared, but the entire department had been eliminated. That meant that forty-five people were instantly laid off. Not only was he stunned for his own future, but he was also deeply concerned about his colleagues and their families. In the conversation with Lynn, Larry let her know about the shock and disillusionment of his team. The company had a reputation for its "cradle to grave" philosophy, and this sudden radical action had created serious emotional trauma. Some of Larry's people had been with the company for more than twenty-six years; this had been their only job, and they had no idea how to cope with the situation. Lynn empathized with Larry's situation and asked him to tell her more. "If money were not an issue, and you could design a program for your team to prepare them to secure new jobs, what would that look like?"

Larry discussed wanting to do something tangible to help prepare his colleagues to face the marketplace with confidence and enthusiasm. He wanted to help them cope with the situation emotionally and strategically. He wanted to equip them with marketing skills and help them create new résumés, apply dress-for-success concepts, and present themselves in successful interviews. He wanted to ensure that they would have jobs and financial security, and be able to create a desirable future that would make them proud and confident.

The corporation financially supported Lynn in assisting Larry with the design of a program to assist all forty-five employees in becoming gainfully employed within sixty days. Lynn turned a situation of lemons into win-win-win lemonade. Not only did she create peace of mind for Larry and jobs for a disenfranchised workforce, but she made an anticipated deficit in revenues into significant additional income for her coaching business. Many of the employees who experienced the "New Beginnings" training that Lynn and Larry designed brought Lynn into their new situation because of the contribution they felt she made. Everyone won! Larry could ethically say "good-bye" to his outstanding team. Lynn got to turn the situation around, and all the employees were hired into great jobs within sixty days!

When you use your listening skills, tune in to what is needed and wanted, respond to the expressed intention, and are fully present in the moment, there is no limit to what you can create. There are unlimited opportunities in each client interaction; if you are paying attention, you will thrive with the abundance of business you can create.

Additionally, there is a marketing aspect to each client relationship. If you are doing an effective job, there should be a natural wellspring of referrals that flows easily from each client. Requesting referrals is perfectly acceptable when it is conducted with ease and elegance. You will develop questions such as, "Who else in your organization might benefit from working with a coach?" or "Whom do you know who would be open to experience coaching with me?" Imagine each client as your marketing ambassador who enthusiastically shares with others the benefits and results they have experienced with your coaching.

CREATING A BUSINESS AND MARKETING PLAN

The process of creating a business plan can easily be obtained for free from various resources on the Internet, for example, www.sba.gov/small businessplanner/. Creating a business plan is a discipline that supports you in articulating your vision and documenting your plan. Your business plan is a road map to your future. The key points you want to address in your business plan are:

1. Definition and description of your business, including the vision, mission, goals, and an explanation of the scope of your services.
2. A marketing plan, including the definition of your market, market analysis, and how to build the bridge between your services and the target market so that you will achieve all of your goals.
3. Sales strategy, including how to inform your target market of what you are offering, competitive analysis, how to close sales, and how to grow your business.
4. A financial plan, including projections for your first three years, how much you charge for each service, how people pay you for your services (cash, check, credit card, PayPal, merchant account, and so on).

Marketing Your Service

The first step in marketing your service is preparing your verbal description of what you do so that the average person on the street can understand what you are saying in plain English or in whatever language you communicate. Take a piece of paper and write out in twenty-five words or less exactly what you are offering, to whom, why they would benefit from your service, and the value you provide. If you were Alberto, you would say, "I help expatriates living in the Netherlands formulate and implement a plan that will provide a fulfilling and satisfying life." In those twenty words, you get a clear picture of what, who, and why. This is also referred to as an elevator speech. It is geared to invite questions and initiate a conversation. The person you are talking to might then ask, "How do you do this?" Alberto's response might be, "I am an MMS trained coach, and I help people sort out their options and preferences to make choices." The potential client might say, "Where do you do this?" Alberto's response might be, "I have an office in my home," or "I come to your location to assess your situation." The purpose of the initial description is to whet the appetite of the person you are talking to, to stimulate curiosity, and to start a dialogue that provides information and will lead to more contacts, presentations, and clients.

After you have completed your initial description, you then design business cards. Your business card needs to include the name of your business, your name and contact information, a logo if you have one, and a tag line that briefly describes your service. Alberto's tag line might be, "Helping expats integrate into Dutch life."

The next step is ordering letterhead, formulating a brochure, and designing a website. Your website is an online brochure that will represent the five *W*s: who, what, where, when, and why. These five *W*s focus and establish your coaching practice. "Who" describes you and differentiates you from other coaches. "What" tells what you are offering and to whom. "Where" informs how to contact you and where you will be conducting your coaching sessions. "When" states the days and times you conduct coaching sessions. "Why" shares your purpose for doing your work. If we use Alberto as the example, the "who" section is a brief biography and positions his credentials as a coach to expats. Alberto's "what" section expands on his tag line, "Helping expats integrate into Dutch life." His "why" section builds a bridge between Alberto and his potential client base, as outlined above.

It is a good idea to use the same words, colors, and fonts on your website as you do in your paper brochure; however, it is not required. You want to choose your image carefully so that as you grow, you build on the brand that you have created. Branding is a science that involves consistency, repetition, and reinforcement. You can execute your marketing plan in stages, but make sure you assign deadlines to each of these steps.

When you have prepared your marketing tools, you can then prepare yourself to meet with prospective clients to present your coaching business so that you become more visible and you get the word out.

The next stage is research. Ask people you know, search online, and target groups or associations that might be interested in what you do. Gather the data and schedule a brainstorming session with friends and supportive family members. Make a list of groups, with the contact person's name and information, and put deadlines on when you will establish contact.

When you initiate contact, determine what level of interest there is, and ask if there is the possibility for you to make a group presentation. Verbally share with everyone you know what you are doing; send out two mailings, e-mail and snail mail, and then schedule a business launch party. Invite people you know well, people you feel are talkative trendsetters who lead the way for others and who can help get the word out, as well as people you would like to be your ambassadors. Do something every day to move your new venture forward, and, if possible, do one significant outreach step per week.

Determining the Value of Your Service

When it comes to setting monetary goals, there are several ways to approach this task. The first is called the "numeric approach." If you follow this method, you determine your monthly expenses, and then back them out to see how many sessions per month, week, and then per day you will need to do to meet them. For example, if your monthly expenses total $4,000, you would divide $4,000 by four weeks and determine that you would need to generate $1,000 per week. You then take $1,000 and divide it by the number of days that you want to be coaching. Let's say that you want to coach five days per week. You would then divide $1,000 by 5 and come up with $200. You would need to generate $200 per day, five days per week, which equals $1,000 per week and totals $4,000 per month. This means that you need to do either two sessions per day at $100 each, or one session per day at $200. When calculating your monthly expenses, don't forget to also include taxes, insurance, and savings.

The second approach is the "intuitive approach." In this method, you pick a number that you feel comfortable with. The number should roll off your tongue without you flinching, blinking, or swallowing. It should be a number that you feel at ease with. This number is the fee that you will charge a client for a coaching session with you. You can go online and gather data to ascertain national coaching fees. In addition, you can query local coaches in your area to find out what they charge. If you choose to do this, take into consideration how long the coach has been coaching and what he or she includes in the coaching session or series of sessions. The price of a coaching session in an urban area will differ from the price in a rural area. Ask yourself what days you want to be coaching; how many clients you want to meet with on any given day; and how much time you would like to have between clients to debrief, make notes, or regroup. Your next step will be to design a program that appears to be compatible with your lifestyle. For example, imagine that you have determined that you want to coach Tuesdays, Wednesdays, and Thursdays, and you want to have three sessions per day at 10:00, 1:00, and 3:00. That would mean that you would have nine sessions per week, totaling thirty-six sessions per month. If you established your starting fees at $100 per session, your gross revenues would be $3,600 per month. If you set your fees at $125, your gross revenues would be $4,500, and if you set your fees at $150, your gross revenues would be $5,400. With this type of schedule you also get to determine how you want to spend the other two days in your week. For example, you could market your services; develop your coaching website; design business cards, brochures, letterhead; network at local organizations; organize and speak about coaching; or meet individually with prospective new coaching clients.

The third approach is called "goal-strategy." With this approach you establish a goal and then map out a strategy. Say you want to have a client base of twenty-four coaching clients. The objective is to locate the people who would be inclined to use your service and sign them up. Frank was a retired CEO who specialized in coaching CEOs. He wanted a total client base of twenty-four heads of companies. He wanted to meet with each client once a month. He made his list of CEOs, drafted his cover letter, created a brochure plus business cards, and sent out his mailing. Then he followed up his mailing with appointments to present the features and benefits to his prospective clients. Since he had been a CEO, he knew exactly the issues they faced and could empathize and support them in their challenges. He possessed the credibility, experience, and reputation, and coupled with his MMS coaching certification, he was a very impressive and compelling coach. Frank also built a DVD library of films that he could assign as homework to his clients. He started to collect articles that were appropriate for CEOs. Frank developed his coaching business targeting the CEO market, and he did his best to supply everything CEOs need and want.

Regardless of which approach you use, you want to be actively promoting your coaching business so that people can benefit from your skills, abilities, and talents. You need to feel comfortable stating your fees, invoicing, and receiving the funds. You also may want to consider offering packages to your clients. For instance, if they sign up for a series of sessions, the price per session is reduced if they pay for all the sessions up front.

You may be a corporate coach, a specialist in your field, or a generalist; however, a big part of your success in the coaching industry is knowing who you are and what you offer, and being crystal clear on the value you provide to your clients. In order to know your value, it is very helpful to be coached by a professional coach. When you have experienced the "other side" of the equation, you will have an enriched perspective. If you have been in the coachee's chair, you have direct experience of how this delicate and precious relationship can be successfully managed. This includes managing expectations, formulating your coaching contract, structuring the frequency of visits, and ensuring the value for revenues invested. While you want to comply with the coaching conventions, you also want to differentiate yourself from other coaches. Determine what makes you special and different from other coaches and what makes you more desirable. Your desirability may be the special packages you offer, the added value you present, or the desirable price point that you propose.

Part of this process involves defining yourself as a coach. Ask yourself these questions: What makes me different? What makes me special? What specifically do I have to offer? What have I done or what do I currently do to justify the fees that I request? Although you may initially respond to these questions with a blank, "I don't know," the answers are incredibly important to your future success. Here's an exercise to help you place a value on your services.

Take a blank piece of paper and on the left-hand side write down all the work and life experiences, certifications, degrees, licenses, accomplishments, years coaching, years involved with each individual endeavor, and anything significant, special, and noteworthy about your capabilities, talents, or life. Then on the right-hand side, place a numerical value. This number represents the value you place on the experience as perceived by a client. After you have listed all of these numbers, you add them together and come up with a total sum of your perceived value of your experience. The numeric value can be between 1 and 100 or can be valued in dollars per hour, per day, or per year. The purpose of the exercise is to derive a way to charge for a service that is very specific and unique. This is a subjective assessment and a starting point. If you were to appraise a house, you would need to start by evaluating the real estate in the close vicinity, called the comparables. Evaluating yourself as a professional coach is similar in that you start by acknowledging the value you provide.

Determining What the Session Includes

You will need to specify what is included in each session and if there is a reduced price when a client signs up for a series of sessions. Many coaches will establish individual coaching packages. You will want to establish your own game rules:

- Will you offer one session or a series?
- Will you require that the client completes assignments? Is there a heavy homework commitment?
- Is there preparation for you, as the coach, to do prior to your sessions?
- Will you provide e-mail contact and/or phone sessions?
- If your office is inconvenient, will you meet in another location where you can concentrate and stay focused on your client?

Remember the questions you encountered in Chapter 1 designed to help you in choosing your own coach? Now it is time for you to answer these questions as a coach. You need to be prepared to answer them because prospective clients could ask any or all of them. When you have completed answering these questions, you will have a better idea of what you are asking from and what you are offering to your clients. Use your responses to create a one-page description of your coaching service. You can amend this whenever you choose, but it will give you a starting point for defining your coaching service.

Take a few minutes to jot down your responses to the following questions:

1. How long have you been coaching?
2. What is the method that you ascribe to?
3. Do you have a specific philosophy or belief system?
4. What approach do you use?
5. What are your coaching assumptions?
6. What are your credentials?
7. Do you have a website, or have you published anything?
8. Are there agreements that you require?
9. What happens if the coachee breaks an agreement?
10. What happens if the coachee doesn't achieve her goals?
11. How long is a session?
12. Do you bill by the session or by the hour?

13. What training did you receive?

14. How many clients do you work with at one time?

15. Do you do phone sessions, face to face, or online chat?

16. Do you assign homework between sessions?

17. What are your expectations of your client?

18. What can your client expect from you?

19. What do you charge? Do you do a series of sessions?

20. Do you take credit cards?

21. Do you take insurance?

22. Do you have a specialty?

23. Can your client speak to other satisfied clients?

24. Do you have availability in the morning, afternoon, or evenings?

25. On what days do you see coaching clients?

ESTABLISHING A NEW CLIENT

Let's imagine that you have set up an introductory interview with a prospective client to address the possibility of coaching with you. The following is the script for an introductory interview. Feel free to change it so that it becomes yours. The purpose of the introductory interview is to explain the coaching process to new clients so that their expectations may be fulfilled, and so they get what they want.

The Introductory Interview

Welcome. My name is _____. Won't you have a seat? Would you like a glass of water?

I would like to know a little about you and give you some information about the coaching process, and then you can ask any questions you may have. Then we can determine if coaching is right for you or not at this time in your growth process. Is that agreeable? Okay. If you don't mind, here is a pad and a pen. If a comment or a question emerges, write it down, and I will address it when I have completed the introduction. Okay?

Before I tell you about coaching, tell me a little bit about you, your situation, and why you are here.

[*The coach listens to the client, and weaves in this information, when appropriate, while completing the presentation.*]

First of all, the coaching process is an everyday approach to problem-solving. It is a client-centered approach to intuitive decision-making. The purpose of the coaching process is to empower you to choose from an inner-directed place a course of action that is "right" for you.

Next I want to address the types of concerns about which people become coached. Coaching challenges are everyday issues like:

- Moving your residence
- Relationship challenges
- Concerns regarding children
- Buying or selling cars
- Financial concerns
- Physical concerns regarding weight or physical fitness
- Creating your home the way you want it
- Job challenges and changes
- Starting a business

. . . and many more. Your coaching session can focus on anything that deals with transition. The situation that you described to me, _____, sounds _____. [*Insert your honest opinion as to whether it seems like a good "item" or not.*]

Coaching is not counseling, nor is it therapy. Coaching is very focused and solution-oriented. If we choose to work together, we enter into a contract of empowerment and support. My job is to get behind you with my intention, my energy, and my belief in your abilities. Your job is to agree to receive the support, to work collaboratively with me, and to communicate fully with me so that we are truly a team.

There are three phases to coaching:

1. Determining your vision, specifically what you want

2. <u>Formulating an action plan to move from here to there</u>
3. <u>Being supported in the realization of the objective</u>

It is difficult to predict how many sessions you may need for any specific concern. There are many factors that come to bear on the duration of an objective. Some of them are:

• How significant the concern is in your life
• How difficult it is for you to come to resolution
• How quickly you want to take action on the issue
• How much self-initiative you are willing to take
• How deep your belief is that you can have what you want
• How much you trust your choices

I will ask you questions about your objective. I will ask you how you feel about it, and what you want. I will ask you probing questions so that you will focus within yourself to find your truth about your issue. We want to make sure that you are true to yourself, your standards, and your values. I may disclose an experience from my own life if it pertains to your situation.

I will *not* give you advice, direction, suggestions, or guidance. It is not my place, nor is it in keeping with the integrity of the process.

As far as our basic assumptions, there are three. The first is that you truly do know what you want. Somewhere within you, underneath the confusion, doubt, uncertainty, and fear, you know what is the "right" thing for you to do in every situation. Second, you possess within you the personal power to have your life be the way you want it to be. Third, you can truly have your life be the way you want it. In all of our interactions, I will be coming from these three core assumptions with you. I will not encourage you to tolerate a situation, make do with undesirable conditions, or convince yourself to compromise yourself, your principles, or your truth.

Let's address some of the practical aspects in the coaching process.

Sessions usually take _____ [*insert time*], and cost
$_____. I am available on these days: _____ at these
times: _____.

I require that you do the following:

- Be on time for sessions.
- Do the assignments.
- Pay at each session or in advance if you choose a package of sessions.
- If you need to cancel, give twenty-four-hour notice; otherwise be financially responsible for the session.
- Keep a notebook or a journal regarding our sessions and your progress.
- Communicate fully to me your reactions, thoughts, and feelings regarding our progress.
- Be committed to getting what you want.

Now, let's address your questions and comments.

[*The coach discusses any questions the client has at this point.*]

How does that sound to you? Do you want to embark on this journey with me as your coach?

Okay, the next steps are:

1. To set up our first session
2. To determine if you want to sign up for a package or a single session
3. For you to complete the Client Information Sheet
4. For you to read and sign the Coaching Contract

Coaching Contract

Dear _____,

(coachee)

  This letter will serve as a coaching agreement between _____ and _____ of _____. This agreement will continue for _____. Each session will be $_____. This will include _____ sessions over the next _____ weeks/months/year. The session will include the coaching session and _____ fifteen-minute follow-up calls between sessions. There will be a weekly report and personal-development assignments between the sessions to ensure program efficiency and progress.

  I am aware that MMS is not therapy and that I will be asked open-ended, probing questions that will assist me in clarifying my goals and objectives. I am aware that I have chosen to negotiate my coaching relationship dates, times, and subjects with my coach.

  I have chosen to enter into a coaching contract with an MMS trained coach. I am clear that the coaching program will not be done to me or for me, and that I alone am responsible for my own experience. If I am not getting what I want, I will ask for clarification and bring any issue to the table, no matter how uncomfortable.

  I am fully aware that all information during the session will be kept strictly confidential.

  All appointments will be charged in full unless there is a twenty-four-hour cancellation notification. If there is a contract termination, a fourteen-day notification is requested along with a conversation about the reasons for that action. I have read and understand all of the points that are in this document. I am in full agreement with the points outlined in this contract.

_____   _____   _____

(coach)   (coachee)   (date)

CHECKING IN WITH YOURSELF BEFORE THE SESSION

Before reviewing your session core competencies, you should check in with yourself. Here are some questions to address. You need to ensure that you are in good shape so that you can support your client. Are you:

• Satisfied with your leadership role?
• Fulfilled with your team role?
• Happy with your job performance?
• Content with your colleagues?
• Prepared to go to the next level?
• Stimulated with your work?
• Peaceful with your life?

The answers to these questions will help you in maintaining objectivity with your clients.

There will be a time when you will schedule your first paid session. This is an exciting moment and you want to be prepared. The following checklist will help you be prepared, focused, and grounded to serve and support your client. Remember how in Chapter 1 we focused on your relationship with yourself? Before you coach, you need to take a few minutes to check in with yourself so that you can dedicate all of your attention to the coachee. Here are six questions that you can ask yourself to get into present time and become fully present.

Mental and Emotional Checklist for Coaching Sessions

1. How do I feel today (physically, emotionally, mentally, spiritually)?
2. What are my thoughts?
3. Is there anything on my mind that might distract me?
4. What have I done to move my projects forward?
5. How do I feel about my progress?
6. Am I choosing to do this session now?

Preparation Checklist for Coaching Session

1. Create a safe, warm, and friendly environment.
2. Turn off or put your phones on vibrate or "hold."
3. Place one clock where only you can see it from your chair.
4. Arrange two chairs and a table in close proximity.
5. Place a pad and pen in the coaching area.
6. Place a box of tissues on the table.
7. Have your Client Information Sheet ready.
8. Do your mental and emotional preparation (as described above).
9. Welcome the client.
10. Ask about use of facilities, desire for water, and so on.
11. Request that the client complete any outstanding paperwork as necessary: contract, information form, etc.
12. Remind client of the confidentiality of the session.
13. Clarify time and outcome expectations.
14. Ask about client's objectives.
15. Start the session.
16. Have your calendar nearby to schedule next session.
17. Be prepared to receive compensation: check/credit card.
18. Renew any compensation agreements.
19. Review your action items.
20. Go over post-action support.

MMS coaches ask, listen, and empower. You need to develop your skills to uncover the hidden truths. It takes practice to master your ability to ask intuitive questions, develop the courage to ask what may seem like obvious or "dumb" questions, and acquire the patience and receptivity for the unanticipated answers. This will require practice over time. Here is a short overview of the coaching progression.

MMS Coaching Session Progression

1. Connection
2. Clarify objective: desired outcome of the session
3. Ask for thoughts and feelings related to the subject
4. Ask for the ideal picture and feelings related to that
5. What is in the way; what is blocking; what is stopping?
6. What do you want to do about it?
7. Restate the objective
8. Intermittently recap the progress
9. Intermittently check on feelings associated with related items
10. Strategy/action step
11. Recapping
12. Closure
13. Support
14. Next steps

CORPORATE CLIENTS HAVE DIFFERENT NEEDS

When a corporation retains your coaching services for their employees, it raises other concerns, particularly in legal matters. Documentation is helpful to both you and to your client. You must always document your sessions with your clients. For instance, in case something adverse happens to the client or to a client's mental health (termination, suicide), you need to be able to track your progress and address what was discussed in any given session. In case there is a legal situation involving your client or their department and you are subpoenaed, you need to be able to refer to your notes. Finally, if there is an internal situation involving ethics, merger, or acquisition and you were called upon as a character reference you will have peace of mind knowing that you are referencing responsible note-taking. Here are the key points involved in corporate coaching to keep in mind.

1. The corporate client is an individual whose sessions are paid for by their organization. Note that there are two levels of accountability.

2. Clients must know what to expect from the coaching experience. Review with them who you are and what you do, and ask them what they expect from coaching.

3. Make certain that you have carefully chosen your meeting place. Be sure that you are sitting in a comfortable location for both of you so that you can conduct the meeting with confidence and confidentiality.

4. Discuss coaching as a profession and address the origin of the profession. In your conversation, address how coaching is different from therapy and consulting.

5. Tell the client about your credentials for conducting corporate coaching.

6. Address the confidentiality and the commitment to them by the coach. All agreements must be clarified up front and established before the contract is signed. The relationship between the client (company), the employee, and the coach is extremely important. There must be clarity and support for all three involved for optimum results.

7. Renew accountability factors and make certain that all three of you are on the same page. Remember, there are two clients to every corporate account and that delicate balance needs to be acknowledged.

8. Establish all future ground rules regarding the placement of coaching in the employee's professional life. Address the level of importance, the consequences for broken agreements, holidays, and changes in logistics and scheduling. Create a twenty-four-hour cancellation policy for all concerned.

9. Create a corporate profile. Make certain you have all of the information you need to stay in touch with your clients.

10. Take copious notes, document sessions, and keep the files in a safe place. Remember to back up your computer files.

❧❦❧

Knowing your talents and needs makes choosing easier. If you choose to embark on your own coaching practice, there are steps to make it work. Marketing is a natural process that expresses your enthusiasm for your endeavors. When you align who you are with what you do, the outcome is increased energy and passion. When others see your "light" and joy shine forth with what you do, they will naturally want some of that energy for themselves.

Coaching Yourself

"How far you go in life depends on your being tender with the young, compassionate with the aged, sympathetic with the striving, and tolerant of the weak and strong. Because someday in your life you will have been all of these."

George Washington Carver

People often ask me the question: Is it possible to coach yourself? The short answer is a qualified "yes." Certain people can coach themselves in certain situations. The challenge of coaching yourself is whether you will be totally honest and can trust your answers. The following questions will help you ascertain whether you could or should consider this: Do you talk yourself out of doing something difficult? Do you rationalize and justify situations to accommodate your feelings and wishes at the moment? Do you hold yourself accountable for what you say you will do? The purpose of coaching is to facilitate choice, to map out a plan, and to support the coachee until the choice is realized. If it is an easy choice, there is no challenge. If it is a difficult choice, one that stretches you outside your comfort zone, then the coaching becomes more difficult. The main factors that impact your ability to coach yourself are fear, considerations, belief in yourself, your capacity to get to the core level of truth underneath the concerns, and your ability to tune in to your essential self. As we discussed in Chapter 1, your relationship with yourself is central to your evolution as a person. If you have a solid, authentic, and positive relationship with yourself, then coaching yourself may be a possibility.

If you have solid character, are a disciplined person, have alignment between the different facets of yourself, and can trust yourself to get to the core truth, then you probably have the capability to coach yourself. Conversely, if you are undisciplined, lack alignment, or believe your own reasons, then you would not be a good candidate for self-coaching. Although difficult to wash your back, it is not impossible. While it is challenging to coach yourself, it is also not completely unfeasible if you are ruthless in getting to the truth. It is probably easier for an introvert to self-coach rather than an extrovert who yearns for interaction with another. It is, however, always a complicated proposition because of several factors:

- If you believe your excuses, reasons, and justifications
- If fear can dissuade you from what you want
- If your old patterns of behavior are stronger than your goals
- If you can't be objective regarding the situation
- If you won't be totally honest and accountable to yourself
- If you won't honor your commitment
- If you can't manage your subpersonalities
- If you don't truly believe in yourself

Let's address each one.

You believe your excuses. Raymond chose to go to Europe for the first time to visit his fiancée who was working abroad on a temporary assignment. He was excited about the trip, planning it, and organizing his things. A few weeks before the date, he started to consider all the things that could go awry. He imagined spending all that time with one person, and feeling the pressure to entertain her and be upbeat all the time. He was concerned that he wouldn't be entertaining or interesting enough. He called Celine to say, "I have changed my mind, and I am not coming." He didn't want to feel insufficient next to Celine, the experienced traveler. She had traveled extensively, spoke French and German, and knew her way around Europe, while he was a rookie. Raymond believed his reservations and lack of confidence had successfully talked himself out of his adventure with his fiancée. In this situation, Raymond would not be a good coach for himself.

Fear dissuades you from what you want. Tonya was asked to go to South Africa to attend a conference and deliver five different speeches. Her initial response was, "Yes, I would love to." As the time drew near, she started to feel nervous. She imagined that she wouldn't be able to meet the expectations. She started to doubt herself, her abilities, and the time allotted to deliver five outstanding speeches. She had given speeches for small groups but never something of this magnitude. Her fear was eclipsing her excitement, and she started to believe the negaholic voice inside her head talking her out of following through with her choice.

Patterns of behavior are stronger than your goals. Samantha was launching a new marketing strategy. As the time grew closer to the launch date, emergencies started to occur, and work became more and more overwhelming with its demands. Samantha felt anxiety from being pulled in every direction. Her tendency was to work harder and longer rather than step back and assess the situation. Left to her own devices, she would lose sight of her priorities. This would keep her in her comfort zone, reinforce her old behavior patterns, and keep her from accomplishing the new venture that would stretch her into a new arena.

You aren't able to be objective. Thomas started graduate school to get his MBA. It sounded like a good idea at the time. He would be able to command a larger salary and would be a more desirable candidate for interesting jobs. In his second semester, he started to think he wasn't cut out for the required math. It was difficult, and he wasn't enjoying his classes. He had lost his objectivity and was suffering from an intense course load that was overwhelming. He went back and forth on a daily basis about whether to stay or to drop out. Thomas's feelings were nudging him in a direction, and he had lost his objectivity.

You aren't accountable to yourself. Let's imagine it is January first, and you have just declared your New Year's resolutions. One of those resolutions is to go to the gym or do some form of exercise three days per week. At this moment you believe this resolution is reasonable, realistic, and attainable. It is now the second week of January, and your boss has instructed you to leave for the Middle East, gather data from three organizations while you are there, synthesize it, return to the United States, and present it at a meeting of the directors, all within five days. You recall your resolution, and in the face of the tasks you have been given, you feel that you must prioritize. For the next ten days, your workouts have been placed on the back burner. Next, you feel tired, and between doing your job, managing your home, and taking care of your family, you have no energy and aren't inspired to go to the gym. You wake up the next morning and have a conversation with yourself about whether you will go to the gym or will sleep in. This is the moment we call "the inner negotiation." The ultimate question is whether you hold yourself to your New Year's resolution or you let yourself off the hook.

You won't stick to your commitment. This is slightly different from being accountable to yourself. Where being accountable relates to your overall goals, sticking to your commitment relates to your daily "to-do" list. There are certain tasks that you must do, and you find yourself resisting them, distracting yourself, or doing everything else other than the task you must do. If you write on your list, "Make twenty cold calls today," and you find yourself organizing your files, inundated with e-mails, or continuously snacking, you might find it difficult to acknowledge the truth to yourself. If you were coaching yourself, you might agree that it is too difficult. You might be sympathetic and offer to go for coffee rather than pick up the phone. You might find a myriad of things to do: research on the Internet, water the plants, organize your in-box, even clean out your desk, rather than face those cold calls. Letting yourself off the hook is something that your coach will not do. If you say you are going to make twenty cold calls, then you will get them done! So in this situation, if you can stay true to your commitment, what you said you would do, then, yes you can coach yourself; if not, then you can't.

You can't manage your subpersonalities. All of us have a variety of facets to our personality. Dr. Candace Pert, author of *Molecules of Emotion,* states that everyone has "subpersonalities." In transactional analysis, the facets are called the *parent,* the *child,* and the *adult.* In other approaches to self-development, the facets are given other names. I like to lovingly call them subpersonalities. There are, of course, various degrees of fragmentation, and if you are severely split, you will require professional help and guidance. If you are aware of your subpersonalities, it doesn't mean that you have a psychiatric disorder; it just means that at some point parts of you either split off or simply never became fully integrated. Here are stories of two people whom I believe would have difficulty if they were to coach themselves.

Alvira had a problem being on time. She is a multifaceted person who lives a busy life. She is an attorney with two children, and she is a fiancée who is busy selling a house and buying a new one in the middle of planning her wedding and honeymoon. Her life is full, and she seems to constantly be running late (although when she needs to be at court, she always manages to get there on time). She also has difficulty getting her bills paid on time, even though she has more than sufficient funds in her account. On the surface, nothing makes sense, yet upon closer inspection and investigation we notice there is more than meets the eye. Alvira is a responsible adult who manages her life as a professional. But lurking within Alvira is a feisty, rebellious, playful, and endearing child named Livie who could care less about being on time or paying bills. For the most part, Alvira runs the show, until Livie gets fed up with all work and no play, pushes Alvira aside, and takes over. The negotiation between Alvira and Livie is interesting, to say the least; however, imagine that Alvira were going to coach herself on the menu at the wedding. Livie's only real interest is in having cake and ice cream, while Alvira would like to have a sit-down dinner with wine. If Livie needed attention, she might dominate, saying, "I don't care about broccoli, fish, or salad. I only want cake and ice cream!" The coaching process could be very difficult without a wedding coordinator who would use her coaching skills to help align Alvira and Livie on the food and beverage for the reception.

Another example of subpersonalities is that of Rafi and Raphael. The differences between the two were obvious. Raphael was a talented artist who specialized in faux painting. The purpose of Raphael's professional life was to astound people with his results so they were happy and delighted with his work. Rafi liked to spend money without regard, party until dawn, go to shows and concerts, and eat and drink as if he would live forever. The discrepancy between the two was that Rafi liked being in control and running things, and it was a strain for Raphael to assert his presence and authority. The relationship between the two of them often felt like a battle. Raphael would insist that the paperwork for the client must be completed, but Rafi would respond, "Chill out. We'll get to it later." If Raphael were coaching himself, he would not be sure whether Rafi or Raphael would surface. The answers and outcomes would be radically different, depending on who was acting as coach.

You don't truly believe in yourself. One of the roles that a coach has is to believe in you more than you believe in yourself, especially when you doubt yourself. If you set your goal on closing ten deals per month, but life gobbles up your time, and you feel like there is no way you can achieve your goal, do you hold your feet to the fire or let yourself off the hook? Believing in yourself means that you have an unswerving trust and confidence in you, so when circumstances become difficult, you stand firm and back your choice absolutely. Belief in yourself is something that you either have or you don't. If you don't have it, it can be developed over time, but it doesn't happen overnight. Belief in yourself is something you are born with, but with repeated and consistent verbal and nonverbal messages that diminish you, the belief in yourself will eventually erode. Rehabilitating this belief in yourself is definitely something you can do. Think of yourself as a garden that has become overgrown with weeds. In order to bring back the beautiful garden, you will need to do some serious weeding to reveal those lovely flowers that lurk underneath. If you want to have back your flowers of belief, you need to start pulling out your first weed. It is a process and will take time, but it is definitely possible.

The Process of Integration

Integration comes from getting your subpersonalities into conversation, into negotiation, and into alignment. Imagine yourself as the grand puppeteer who has a variety of marionettes at your disposal. You need to be senior to the various facets of your personality. You need to be able to manage the various parts of you that might pull you in different directions. If there is a part of you that wants to walk on the wild side, you need to attend to that in a safe way so that you don't put yourself or your family at risk. Your job is to manage the personalities as the CEO of your life. Whether your subpersonalities urge you to eat sugar, smoke cigarettes, or act out sexually, you need to be able to manage them, so they are placated and don't get you into uncomfortable situations. Take, for example, famous professional athletes and actors who have experienced negative publicity because of their various addictions to drugs, alcohol, gambling, and sex. You would imagine that with the wealth and power that these celebrities have, they could discreetly handle their addictions. It is the subpersonalities that take over in these instances and become senior to the person. In your own life, make sure that your subpersonalities are in check so they don't lead you down a path of negative attention and reinforcement.

How I Coached Myself and Developed the MMS Process

In 1974, I was experiencing a premature midlife crisis. I had become a teacher to please my mother. She passed away when I was twenty, and then I became an actress for myself. I left the theater when I discovered that I could not bear being unemployed for long periods of time. I didn't know what I should do, and I didn't know where to turn for answers. When I shared with friends that I was trying to figure out what I was supposed to do with my life, I received a plethora of suggestions and good ideas. From a real-estate agent to a lawyer, to a doctor, to a vitamin salesperson, I was inundated with people's thoughts about what I could or should do. Although they were all well-meaning, it exacerbated my confusion, and I was in a conundrum. At the peak of my confusion, I had an insight to turn within. I devoted three months of my life determined to find my purpose, passion, and power. I started making lists, meditating, and praying. I asked for guidance, and I wrote down everything that I discovered about myself. In that three months, I found the work I have been doing since 1974. I created the MMS coaching process. I connected with my higher self, received my messages, and aligned my energies toward supporting people in making their visions, dreams, and goals become reality. In a very real sense, you could say that I coached myself during that period. I set aside the time, declared my objective, and set out to accomplish it. I believe it is because I am an introvert and didn't know where else to turn that I turned within, structured my time, listened to my messages, and started the process. It is this process that I did with myself that we make available to our students who want to become MMS certified coaches. It worked with me, and it has worked with thousands of others over the decades. Now let's address using the MMS method to coach yourself.

COACHING YOURSELF

When you shift to being both the coach and the coachee, there are some logistical questions to ask: Do you switch from one chair to another? Do you write one question in blue and answer it in green? Do you look in the mirror and ask a question looking into your right eye, and then respond looking into your left eye? You must see what method works for you if you are going to coach yourself, and then set up the coaching session in a formal manner, just as you would with a paying client. Let's address some requirements. In order to coach yourself, you must:

- Know yourself very well.
- Know what you do to kid, fool, or deceive yourself.
- Know what tactics you use to camouflage the truth from yourself.
- Know how to get yourself back on track when you want to quit.
- Know how to cut through your own resistance.
- Know how to support yourself when you don't want it.

Establish where, when, what, and how long to ensure that you are setting out on a structured, scheduled, and focused approach. In addition, you also want to know what underlying beliefs might be blocking you from achieving your goals. For instance, if you have the belief, "I can never get what I want," that concept could defeat your efforts.

Belief	Behaviors	Reality Construct
I create my life.	Results	I will make my life wonderful.
I'm the designer of my own life.	Creative	I want to manifest my dreams. . . .
You can create your own reality.	Proactive	If I could, I would cause my results. . . .
We will find a way.	Resolved	Let's do it!

Obstacles can be overcome.	Reconciled	There must be a way.
Take what you get and make the best of it.	Responsive	Since I have this, I will . . .
You can't get what you want.	Resigned	I must accept my plight.
Life is tough.	Reactive	I must fight to keep what I have.
I can't trust anyone.	Resistant	I'll do it my way.
I am all alone.	Reclusive	I can only count on me.

The underlying belief drives the behavior, and creates the reality around which you construct your life. If you are locked into a belief that doesn't support your goal, you need to bring it to the surface, tell the truth about it, and address what you are going to do about it before the session. Coaches can usually flush out underlying unconscious beliefs. If you are to coach yourself, you need to be able to unearth the unseen drivers of behavior. For example, if you are single and keep trying to find your soul mate, but nothing seems to work, your underlying belief might be, "I will never find someone who is a match for me. There is no one out there!" If this is your belief, no amount of introductions, no Internet dating services, no singles mixers will enable you to overcome that belief, and you will ultimately be right that you will never find that person. The question you must ask yourself is: Am I ruthless enough to unearth the unconscious underlying beliefs that are keeping me from what I want? If the answer is "yes," then go for it.

Formulating Your Life Compass

Let's start at the first moment of awareness that you have personal choices to make: young adulthood. Somewhere between the ages of eighteen and twenty-five, you must determine what you are going to do with your life. The questions that surface are: Do you stay in school and get an advanced degree? Do you get a job? Do you secure a combination of school and job? Do you get married and start a family? Do you launch into a combination of school and family or job and family? Do you go traveling?

Each one of us must determine what we are going to do with our lives. For some people, this is an easy process. For others, it becomes a real challenge. Whether the path is outlined for you or you must sort it out for yourself, it is something that each one of us must come to terms with sooner or later. Whether you do this process with a coach or you do it with yourself, it must be done. If you haven't already examined this process, you will want to see what is true for you about formulating your life compass.

Family expectations. The first way to determine one's life path is based on parental influence. Your parents may have very specific ideas on who you should be, what you should do, who you should marry, how many children you should have, your religious affiliation, and your political proclivity. You could either align yourself with your parents' expectations or you could do the exact opposite, but either way the major catalyst for this type of scenario is your parents. Most likely, if parental influence is your main driver, the expectations you experience are probably the reflection of your parents' choices and values or the polar opposite.

Extended family and valued friends. The second way of determining one's path is similar to the first, but expands to include extended family, friends, teachers, and sports coaches, and is about fulfilling external expectations of valued friends. If you excel at a particular sport, a coach might encourage you to apply for an athletic scholarship. If you have demonstrated other abilities, you might well be encouraged to pursue those talents.

Heroes and role models. In addition to family and friends, many young people have heroes, "sheroes," or role models. These larger-than-life people frequently become an inspiration for someone's career. Whether the inspiration comes from a friend, a teacher, or a celebrity, it emanates from a respected and valued person.

Chance opportunities. Another way is for an opportunity to be presented by a family member, friend, acquaintance, or by reading an ad in the paper. When an opportunity is presented and accepted, a process begins. For instance, you have completed your school term and are offered a summer job that you accept. The job may not be exactly what you'd imagined you were looking for, but it may be a short-term solution to your immediate employment needs. Sometimes people forget that the job was part of a short-term plan, and they end up staying at that one job for a very long time because it becomes familiar, predictable, and comfortable.

Career trends. An additional way is when the overall environment changes so dramatically that it impacts your career choice. Career trends shift depending upon supply, demand, and what's popular at the moment. As technology became more integrated into daily life, it became a more desirable career choice. What is perceived as "a career for the future," or what career counselors are encouraging at the time, may create an upsurge in certain fields.

Monetary drivers. Some people's highest priority is making money. They therefore focus on how to make the most amount of money and formulate their career plans according to that one stipulation. With the focus on consumerism and celebrities, many young people's highest priority is earning power.

Least resistance. Some people are in search of the least amount of hassle and stress and choose the path of least resistance. Others like to get into "life's boat" and see where it takes them. They want to go with the flow and be surprised at what turns up. Others want to find their mate and procreate because that is their highest value. Next to that, everything else is secondary.

Intrinsic values. There is another way of formulating your life compass—getting to get to know yourself through awareness, reflection, determining preferences, prioritizing, meditation, and creating a vision of your life from the inside out. We call this process "formulating inner-directed options and choices."

TYPES OF SESSIONS YOU CAN DO WITH YOURSELF

In the following section, I offer some tools and techniques that will guide you on your path to self-coaching. These exercises and tasks have been tested by people of both genders, in various professions, in different countries, for over three decades. They really work quite effectively if you take the time to do them. Even if every exercise doesn't resonate, look for ones that you are willing to complete or that are workable into your schedule.

Sorting Out Priorities

There are a variety of ways that people determine what is right for them. Choices and decisions may be based on capabilities, preferences, expectations, limitations, geography, economics, passion, or following in another's footsteps. Main drivers may be intrinsic or extrinsic. You can do this process with yourself to see what is most important to you. You may see the same answer surface in several places, and if it does, it means that you need to take note. To start the process, complete these statements:

1. I enjoy these activities . . .
2. I like spending my time . . .
3. I am good at . . .
4. I feel fulfilled when I . . .
5. The situations that give me joy and energy are . . .
6. These things are important to me . . .
7. If I didn't have any financial concerns, I would . . .
8. The things that I truly want to do are . . .

9. The things that bring me satisfaction are . . .

10. I feel peaceful and purposeful when I . . .

It is important to gravitate toward those activities and aspects that bring you energy, a feeling of value and worth, and make you feel like your best self. It is also important to note the difference between those things that bring you joy and those items that cause you stress. Here is another set of statements to complete:

1. People who drain my energy are . . .

2. Activities that rob me of my vitality are . . .

3. I feel unmotivated when I . . .

4. The things that make me feel out of balance are . . .

When you sort out the motivators from the "de-motivators," you will have a better idea of where to point your life compass.

Taking Inventory

On the first of every month, you can take inventory of your life. This is a simple exercise you can do with yourself, a piece of paper, and a pen. Draw a line down the center of the paper. The heading on the left is: "What Could Improve," and the heading on the right is: "What's Working." Then download all of the things in your life that either need work or are working for you. There is no particular order to the list. You can include small things and large things; the size of the item doesn't matter. If it comes up as an item to list, then it is important to you. You could include your relationship with your son, your car, your boss, your hair, your weight, your job, and your home—whatever could be either bothering you or pleasing you. If the list is the same month after month, you can conclude that you are stuck. As you take your personal inventory at the beginning of each month, you can track your progress and see if you are growing or if you've stopped. You can do this in your journal and track progress throughout the year. At the end of the year, you can review your overall growth and accomplishments for the year.

The "I Want" Exercise

When you are confused and hear yourself saying, "I don't know what I want," take a blank piece of paper, write "I want" at the top, and date it. Then, while suspending judgment, write out as many of your wants as you can imagine, and do it as quickly as you can. Don't sit and ponder—just write. After you have completed listing all of your wants, review them to see which ones you want to act on. This exercise activates your desires, doesn't take long, and is very effective and efficient.

Acknowledgments

I wrote about the importance of acknowledgments in *Negaholics: How to Overcome Negativity and Turn Your Life Around,* but in case you haven't seen that book, I want to emphasize the importance of shining the spotlight on the good news, and on what you are doing "right." If your relationship with yourself could use a boost, if you tend to dwell on what didn't get done, or you take for granted what you did get done, then this is the perfect exercise for you. Before you brush your teeth tonight, write down ten good things that happened today. Don't just think of them—write them down. The reason you write them is for the triple positive imprint. When you write them, you hear them in your head, you see them on the paper, and you experience them kinesthetically as your hand moves across the page. After you write them, read them to yourself. Ten acknowledgments a day keep the beat-ups away! If you tend to beat yourself up, do acknowledgments every night without fail.

Life-Line Process

The life-line process is a fun and interesting exercise that you can do with yourself or with a client. It usually is a good choice when someone indicates that he or she wants to do many things and is having difficulty making the choice of just one. First, take a blank sheet of paper and list on it everything you want to do before you die. Include professional items, personal wishes, and dreams. After you have a thorough list of everything you could possibly imagine that you want to do before you transition, take a piece of paper, as large as possible, and draw a diagonal line from the bottom left to the top right. At the bottom left write your current age. At the top right write the age at which you would ideally like to pass on. This doesn't need to be accurate, of course; you are just using a number for the exercise. The higher the number, the more things you get to add to your life line. Next, review your list of "lifetime to-dos," select one, and put it on the life line with an age next to it. Do this until you have added all of the items on your list. If there is not enough time to complete everything, either change some of the years, or extend the life line longer. When you have completed this, review your life line to see how it looks and feels. Ask yourself: Did I do everything I wanted to do? See if there is anything missing. If there is, add it in the appropriate place. If you see that you don't really want to include something that is listed, just delete it. The purpose of the exercise is to create a map or timeline in which you get to do it all. Rather than have it swirling around in your head, you now have it on paper and can refer to it whenever you want.

Visioning Process

You can do a visioning process with yourself or with a client. It is a simple exercise that invites your imagination to guide you on your journey. Visioning exercises are usually done with your eyes closed. You get into a comfortable position, away from noise and distractions. You turn off your phone and ask others in the area to let you be for approximately fifteen minutes. Then you go into a state of deep relaxation, starting at the top of your head, going through your body, taking deep breaths and releasing any tension or pressure. As you reach your feet and let go of the last vestiges of tension, you will be ready to begin the exercise. Imagine yourself waking up at peace, with a big smile on your face. You are happy and fulfilled, rested and stimulated, and doing everything you love to do. Today is a perfect day, and you can have everything your way. What is the first thing you do? What do you do next? The rules of this process are if you are not enjoying what you're envisioning, change the scenario, change the picture, change the people, and make it your ideal vision.

As the process unfolds, it will become apparent whether this is a workday or a day of leisure. If it is a free day, don't worry; just transition into the next day that naturally becomes a workday. The idea is to get at those elements that give you a sense of joy, satisfaction, fulfillment, and peace. The reason this exercise is usually done with eyes closed is because you go inside and start to allow your imagination to unravel and give you clues to your life puzzle. Without the pressure of saying the right thing or knowing the answers, your imagination can reveal what it is holding as important, precious, and desirable.

After the visioning process is complete, write down the key points of discovery. Just like waking up from a dream, you want to capture it before it fades away. If you are conducting a visioning exercise with a client, document what they are saying while they are speaking. The relevant nuggets from the exercise may be the scenario that is envisioned, the qualities of the experience, or specific elements that are present.

A visioning exercise I conducted with Lydia was interesting in that she didn't radically change any of the elements of her work; however, she did change the location of her office. She had always had her office in the heart of New York City, where she believed it needed to be for the publishing world. In the visioning exercise, she said she wanted to be in the country rather than in the city. This vision surprised her, and it required her to stretch her idea of where her business needed to be physically located. She wanted to be within commuting distance from New York so that she could reach the city for meetings, and she wanted to be able to escape by train at a moment's notice. She wanted her base of operations to be surrounded by trees, grass, and sunlight. She wanted to feel connected to nature, to hear the wind rustling in the trees, and to smell the scent of freshly cut grass. The yearning she felt was undeniable. Shortly after the session, she started to look for homes and nearby offices that had those qualities. She found the perfect location that made her heart sing. She is still doing the work she has done for several decades, but now she does it with the peaceful smile of satisfaction and renewal on her face.

What's True About Me?

This is an ongoing exercise. In a special place that you will never lose, list what is true about you. This list can change over time as you grow and develop. List whatever is true about you now. The list can include your qualities, preferences, proclivities, whatever you think is true about you at this time. You can even include whether you are able to coach yourself or not. This document is important because when life throws you a curve ball and you can't remember what you like or what you want, it reminds you of who you were at that time. Remember, you always have choices, and if you want to change anything on the list, you always have that option. Knowing yourself is the first step to becoming a "brilliant" coach.

❧❦❧

Coaching yourself is not impossible, but it does have its challenges. If you have the desire, willingness, belief, and commitment, you can make this happen. It is always good to have external accountability to ensure that you are operating with integrity, being totally honest with yourself, and going for what you truly want.

Creating Community

10

"A community needs a soul if it is to become
a true home for human beings. You, the people,
must give it this soul."

Pope John Paul II

W hen I was a child, I was especially touched by the story *The Wizard of Oz*. In the story, Dorothy travels down the yellow brick road looking for home. On her journey, she meets the scarecrow who is in search of a brain. They team up, and down the road they find a tin man who yearns for a heart. He joins the other two, and farther down the road, they stumble upon a lion, who it turns out is longing for courage. Each one is searching for some part of themselves that they feel is missing. Because they have all admitted their deficiencies, there is a lot of empathy and support for each other. As they travel down the yellow brick road, they encounter adversity, challenges, and obstacles. Through their determination, teamwork, and commitment to get what they want, they overcome all of the difficulties and persevere to the end of their journey. They are all quite different, their wishes are all diverse, and their capabilities vary greatly; however, they band together, capitalize on their strengths, focus on their common goal of getting to Oz, and support each other in getting what they want. This model for living implanted itself into Lynn's and my psyches at a young age. In 1974, Lynn and I set out to create a similar reality for people through our organization, The MMS Institute. Our Inner Negotiation Workshop is like the yellow brick road. Diverse people come with various objectives, and through the group process everyone gets to Oz, the realization of their dreams. Whether they want to find their hearts, to discover their brains, to reveal their courage, to find their way back "home," or something else, all things are possible. We invite them to believe, to trust, and to overcome the obstacles, challenges, and adversities they experience. At MMS, we specialize in making dreams come true. The experience is magical, and since the facilitators are MMS certified coaches, they naturally want to support and empower all of the participants in achieving all of their objectives.

When you experience what it feels like to be respected, supported, and valued, you start to become your authentic self and open up the door for unlimited possibilities. When you feel safe enough to tell your truth, encouraged to imagine and explore, and urged to believe in yourself, you want everyone to be introduced to this way of life. It is not a religion, nor is it a cult; it is a way of life that is optimistic, hopeful, and empowering. When you propose a new idea, rather than facing the traditional devil's advocate espousing all the reasons that you can't or shouldn't do it, you are instead invited to explore the possibilities. No idea is a bad idea, and underneath each twinkling of an eye resides the seed of inspiration. Inventors are those who dream of something that doesn't yet exist. They all have vision, courage, dedication, and perseverance. They take initiative, solve problems, and work hard to invest their time, energy, and money in their dreams. You are probably familiar with the biographies of the Wright brothers, Thomas Edison, Albert Einstein, Leonardo da Vinci,

Benjamin Franklin, Johannes Gutenberg, Galileo Galilei, Isaac Newton, Samuel Morse, Eli Whitney, Guglielmo Marconi, and George Washington Carver who changed the world and the way we live our lives. Every day we have visionaries, inventors, and entrepreneurs who are willing to challenge the status quo. You may very well be the midwife to help birth a new idea, invention, or vision in one of your coaching sessions. For each idea to come into existence, it must find a fertile place to grow. The safety that you provide for someone who was previously ridiculed for an idea might be just what is needed to encourage that invention to come into existence. Remember the ridicule that the Wright brothers experienced? Imagine them coming to you for a coaching session about their flying machine. At any time, in any location, someone could be sitting across from you with a wish or a dream that could change the world. The coaching process has the capacity to open up unimaginable doors and make seemingly impossible things happen.

Imagine a world where people listen to what you have to say because they are sincerely interested. Consider a world where people seriously want each other to win and do their best to support each other through life's adverse lessons.

When you live the coaching process that we teach at MMS, you don't necessarily fit into the world of convention, but rather connect with your own purpose and align yourself with your value system and principles. When you live the process, you are committed to fulfillment rather than the trappings of success. You are dedicated to authenticity rather than position, prestige, or perks. You are devoted to the truth and honoring your ultimate purpose in life rather than momentary appetite gratification. It is because you have this unswerving allegiance to connection, meaning, and the deeper values in life that you have the ability to support your clients, colleagues, and friends in being loyal to their higher selves. When you live the process, you encourage, empower, and enkindle joy in others, aligning them with their true essence and values.

Coaching is a positively contagious process where people who are winning in life want to be surrounded by other winners. This is the reason building community is a natural outgrowth of the coaching process and the coaching relationship. Building community is a strategic approach that involves reaching out to people and offering support. You want to include those people who are important to you, with whom you would like to connect on a deeper level, and with whom you want to be actively playing the game of support and empowerment along with you and the other coaches.

Building community means that people share certain values, mores, customs, and ascribe to similar behaviors. Building community requires shared interests.

The question has been asked, "Can you coach anyone?" The answer is "yes," as long as they:

- Have a specific objective, something they want
- Are ready, willing, and able to get clear on it (now)
- Know that they will formulate their own answers to the challenges they are facing

That being said, some people are easier to coach than others. The more evolved people are, the easier they are to coach—unless they are infected with spiritual arrogance, which fills them with righteousness that is next to impossible to coach because they "know it all." As I stated above, some, more than others, are able to reach outside the social norms, evaluate their behaviors and circumstances, and consciously make their own choices and changes. They are more "evolved" when it comes to deliberately deviating from the norm. The following is an Evolutionary Scale of Life Conditions, which helps gauge how ready a person is to connect with their own purpose instead of with the world of convention. The scale starts in the middle at zero and reads both up and down from the zero point. Zero represents a base line of "okayness." The person at zero is not suffering, nor are they flourishing. The person at zero is functional and adequate. The people who are above zero or "above the line" will be easier to coach than those below zero or "below the line." The reason for this is the higher their positive number is on the scale, the more in touch they are with a desire to empower themselves and make their own conscious choices, which is a crucial starting point for any coach and coachee.

Evolutionary Scale of Life Conditions

7 = Inner peace

6 = Able to manifest life purpose

5 = Pursuing health and wellness on all levels

4 = Contributing to society

3 = Designing a life path

2 = Believing that choices are available and exploring them

1 = Taking responsibility for one's life

0 = Stable/neutral

-1 = Not in control of circumstances

-2 = Blaming others for wrong choices/powerlessness/playing victim

-3 = Addiction or overusing/overdependence

-4 = Unemployed, in financial distress, not a functioning part of society

-5 = Depressed and/or chronically ill

-6 = Lacks sense of meaning and desire to manifest life purpose

-7 = Anxious, fearful, debilitated, feeling stuck and paralyzed

COACHING IS POSITIVELY INFECTIOUS

Once you start to grow and succeed in one area of your life, you then start to ask yourself if the same principles could be applied to other areas. If you are winning at work, why couldn't you have a healthy, positive, loving, and supportive relationship? If your relationship is flourishing, then why can't you have a home that supports you? If your home has become your sanctuary, then why can't you have a healthy body? If your body is healthy, fit, and functioning at optimum performance, then why can't you manage your time more effectively? If management of your resources is in alignment with your values, then why not expand to include your family relationships? If your relationships with family members are authentic, connected, and empowering, then why not expand that to include your circle of friends? If your circle of friends is solid and true, then why not expand that to include your community? Expanding the circle of support in concentric circles allows you to be yourself, support others in their dreams and goals, and be empowered by others in all of your endeavors as well. In a perfect world, everyone you know would choose to follow your lead into the light of unlimited possibilities. Since we don't live in a perfect world, we need to have alternatives if people in our extended families and circle of friends don't choose our values.

There have always been and will always be people who don't want to grow, who don't want to invest the time, energy, and money to better themselves; there will always be people who don't believe they can have what they want, who think they're fine as they are, who believe they are self-sufficient and don't need others to help them. These people may be willing to cross over the threshold to a world of new possibilities, or they may be unwilling and simply say, "no." The division between those who are willing and eager to grow and those who aren't has been around since the evolution of the *Homo sapien*. Plato wrote his "Analogy of the Cave" in book VII of *The Republic*, where he described a similar phenomenon. Here we have a brief excerpt of what Plato wrote nearly 2,400 years ago:

> *Imagine prisoners who have been chained since childhood deep inside a cave. Not only do the chains immobilize their limbs; their heads are chained as well, so that their gaze is fixed on a wall. Behind the prisoners is an enormous fire, and between the fire and the prisoners is a raised walkway, along which people carry statues of various animals, plants, and other objects. The statues cast shadows on the wall, and the prisoners watch these shadows. When one of the statue-carriers speaks, an echo against the wall causes the prisoners to believe that the words come from the shadows.*
>
> *The prisoners engage in what appears to us to be a game: naming the*

shapes as they come by. This, however, is the only reality that they know, even though they are seeing merely shadows of images. They are thus conditioned to judge the quality of one another by their skill in quickly naming the shapes and dislike those who begin to play poorly.

Suppose a prisoner is released and compelled to stand up and turn around. At that moment his eyes will be blinded by the firelight, and the shapes passing will appear less real than their shadows.

Similarly, if he is dragged out of the cave into the sunlight, his eyes will be so blinded that he will not be able to see anything. At first, he will be able to see darker shapes such as shadows and, only later, brighter and brighter objects. The last object he would be able to see is the sun, which, in time, he would learn to see as that object which provides the seasons and the courses of the year, presides over all things in the visible region, and is in some way the cause of all these things that he has seen. Once enlightened, so to speak, the freed prisoner would not want to return to the cave to free "his fellow bondsmen," but would be compelled to do so. Another problem lies in the other prisoners not wanting to be freed: descending back into the cave would require that the freed prisoner's eyes adjust again, and for a time, he would be one of the ones identifying shapes on the wall. His eyes would be swamped by the darkness, and would take time to become acclimated. Therefore, he would not be able to identify shapes on the wall as well as the other prisoners, making it seem as if his being taken to the surface completely ruined his eyesight.

Philosophers are like the man who escapes from the cave and sees the real world. If you are reading this book, you are what Plato called a "philosopher." Plato lived in 400 BC, but this passage is relevant today since there continue to be people who want to stay in the darkness of the cave, look at the shadows, and believe the shadows are real, rather than question the norms, break out of the shackles, and risk going into the light. Some people will be happy to know that there is another way to live, while others will resist, resent, and refuse to deviate from the familiarity of what they know. The choice of upward spiral or downward corkscrew is available to each one of us. The upward spiral of positive living sounds natural and easy; however, remember the average person lives an unexamined life riddled with habits, patterns, and addictions. I spent some time researching what constitutes "the norm," and I discovered twenty factors that constitute "the norm" in people in the United States today. They aren't good, bad, right, or wrong; they are some factors that are consistently true of the average person. Don't be alarmed if you identify with one or more characteristics; just notice how many are true for you. The characteristics of the average person are:

1. Eats fast food at least twice per week
2. Watches seven or more hours of TV per day
3. Shops in malls at least once per week
4. Drinks a minimum of three cups of coffee per day
5. Drinks a minimum of two carbonated beverages daily
6. Has credit card debt (at least $9,000)
7. Takes some form of prescribed medication
8. Is at least thirty pounds overweight
9. Owns and uses a cell phone without any Electro Magnetic Frequency protection
10. Eats some form of refined sugar daily
11. Reads tabloids or celebrity magazines
12. Gambles (at least on sports or on the lottery)
13. Drives a car with a V-8 engine or a truck
14. Buys brand-name products
15. Listens to advertising
16. Lives vicariously through celebrities' lives
17. Has at least a high-school education
18. Earns approximately $30,000 per year
19. Suffers from at least one addiction
20. Has essentially stopped learning anything new

People who possess a majority of these characteristics are part of the social norm, follow the crowd or the trends, and do what they are told.

They are like Plato's cave dwellers who accept the reality they are given. The point of this exercise is not to put a negative connotation on the social norm. The point is, however, to ask whether or not you are consciously choosing to partake in these behaviors. If you are consciously making choices to—or not to—practice these "norms," and no outside source is dictating your decisions, then you are more than ready and "evolved" to begin a journey to manifest your own destiny. However, so many times when we do this exercise in MMS workshops, many people gasp when they discover that they have been unconsciously participating in these "norms" and determine that they should be more mindful. This exercise in consciousness and being aware of what your realty is, which is sometimes different from the reality that is dictated to us by society, is a major step in coming out of Plato's proverbial cave and leading people into building a community of unlimited possibilities.

In order to build your community, you need to be able to:

• Reach out to others without judgment.
• Open the door of possibility without agenda.
• Invite, encourage, and inspire without attachment.
• Assess and include if they are willing.
• Move on with no regret if they are unwilling.

Imagine your community embracing the Twelve Steps to Living the Process, as outlined in Chapter 7. Imagine everyone you know doing what they love, honoring their feelings, telling their truth, looking within for guidance and direction, focusing on solutions, and believing in themselves and each other. Imagine them being committed to growing, loving themselves and each other unconditionally, pursuing their dreams, listening to their messages, reaching out to others for support, being responsible for their actions, looking at everything as a mirror, learning lessons, and continually growing. When that reality surrounds you, you start to live a very different life, one that activates your higher consciousness, the quest for innovation, for the noblest part, and that part that wants to contribute. This is a very different type of human than we see portrayed on TV or in the movies.

In 1977, I wrote a book titled *The New Species: A Vision of the Evolution of the Human Being*. I wrote the book as a text for our MMS Coach Training. I thought it would be the only book I would ever write. I didn't think of myself as an author, but I wanted to get the information into the hands of the participants, and so I self-published the book. In *The New Species*, I present the concept of raising a new generation that is as evolved in consciousness as Darwin described our physical evolution from the apes. From the way we give birth, educate, and parent our children, we have the capacity to elevate their awareness so that even the thought of killing one of our own species would be unimaginable. Instead of slaying and conquering for whatever "noble" reason, humans will derive ways to work together to improve conditions for the good of the whole.

Global warming is one of these conditions that invites us to work together for the good of the planet. Not only does this issue impact every person on the Earth, but it also will affect all future generations. What an opportunity to transcend our differences, to leap beyond economics, and to find ways for us to solve the problems we have created. Consider coaching applied to global warming. Imagine the coaching model allowing us to invent solutions to our current dilemmas.

The applications for coaching are endless. You can expand the scope from the individual to the family, to the community, to the country, to the continent, to the world. You have inside you the seeds for greatness, and you can make a difference. Consider this . . .

Consider that you were put on Earth for a reason. Consider that there are no accidents. Consider that you are here to help individuals with their challenges. Consider that you are here to help people resolve their differences. Consider that you can help solve the problems that we face today: poverty, hunger, disease, corruption, pollution, global warming, and war. Consider that in your presence, someone may birth an idea whose time is ripe and that will help solve our many problems. Consider that you are more magnificent than you ever imagined and that you possess the power to help those who need to illuminate their answers. Consider that you are wise, powerful, and ethical beyond your wildest dreams. Consider that being alive at this moment in time is no accident. Consider being all of who you are, and allowing your greatness to manifest.

⚜

Coaching creates consciousness. Every time you coach another person, you enable their inner light to shine. As the light grows, it reveals what has been hidden in the darkness. When lights gather together, community is created. When you create community, you reinforce the world's unlimited possibilities, manifestation, and miracles.

When you listen to your inner wisdom, you become evolved. When you trust yourself, you become a leader. When you believe all things are possible, you become a visionary. When you are willing to fulfill your purpose on Earth, you are enlightened. When you leave the planet better than you found it, you are a self-actualized being.

Love yourself, trust your choices, and know that everything is possible!

The Living Language of Coaching

Abundance. Consider that there is more than enough for everyone.

Acceptance. Embrace what life offers you with a positive attitude.

Accountability. Acknowledge that you are at cause and answerable for your actions.

Adventure. Live with a spirit of joy and enthusiasm.

Affirmation. Positively state the truth as you intend it to manifest.

Awareness. Be fully conscious in the moment.

Balance. Intentionally allocate effort to create equilibrium and harmony.

Beliefs. The unconscious expectations that dictate your behavior.

Causality. Acknowledge that you are the source of your manifestations.

Choice. Explore your preferences, and then select your action.

Clarity. See people and things as they really are.

Commitment. Devote yourself to something or someone, and honor that choice—no matter what.

Communication. Form a bridge between you and another.

Completion. Unleash your ability to get things done.

Courage. The inner strength required when confronting danger, difficulty, or opposition.

Creativity. Allow your imagination to bring something into existence.

Enthusiasm. Eagerly express and demonstrate your interest.

Ethics. Doing the right thing, especially when no one is watching.

Fairness. Perceive things as equitable, and then anticipate justice prevailing.

Faith. Believe without tangible proof that something is so.

Freedom. Give yourself permission to do what you want.

Goals. Formulate markers that acknowledge your progress and show you where energy or effort is needed.

Grace. Be fully in tune with your spiritual essence, sustained by a higher power.

Gratitude. Discover the blessings you already have.

Guidance. Allow and empower someone you trust to guide you on your path.

Healing. Restore yourself to a state of well-being.

Honesty. Disclose your truth without altering it.

Humility. Be confident and modest about your own merits, and understand your limitations.

Humor. Laugh at your shortcomings.

Inspiration. Listen to the spirit within.

Integrity. Live by a set of personal values that enhance your life.

Intimacy. Allow another inside your thoughts, feelings, perceptions, fears, wishes, hopes, and dreams.

Kindness. Do considerate acts without an agenda.

Limitlessness. Live without restrictions or limitations.

Listening. Actively focus on the information you're receiving.

Love. Embrace another in their totality, and support them in all their dreams.

Loyalty. Develop an unshakable allegiance to something or someone.

Openness. Be receptive to what happens, and consider seeing it as necessary for your growth.

Patience. Display tolerance while awaiting outcomes.

Pleasure. Physically manifest your joy.

Power. Demonstrate your ability to manifest reality.

Respect. Hold yourself and others in high regard.

Responsibility. Admit your accountability; acknowledge your influence and role.

Self-esteem. Feel worthy and able to meet all of life's challenges.

Success. Live in alignment with your values, visions, abilities, and potential.

Support. Provide reinforcement and strength for yourself and others.

Surrender. Transcend your ego and release control.

Tolerance. Outwardly express your acceptance of others.

Transformation. Decide how you want to positively change yourself.

Trust. Know who and what you can count on.

Wisdom. Access your highest and deepest degree of knowledge, insight, and understanding.

Index

193

About the Authors

New York Times #1 bestselling author **Chérie Carter-Scott, Ph.D.**, has been coaching change successfully since 1974. Dr. Carter-Scott is an international author, entrepreneur, consultant, lecturer, teacher/trainer, talk-show host, and seminar leader. Her company, Motivation Management Service (MMS) Institute, Inc., has reached millions of people worldwide. Dr. Carter-Scott's Fortune 500 corporate clients include: AMI, FMC, American Express, IBM, GTE, State Farm Insurance, SGI, Burger King, and *Better Homes and Gardens* magazine.

Dr. Carter-Scott has promoted her books across the world, including appearances on national programs such as *The Oprah Winfrey Show, Leeza Live, Iyanla, The Other Half, The Montel Williams Show, Jenny Jones, The Sally Jesse Raphael Show, Politically Incorrect, The Today Show, The O'Reilly Factor*, and more than five hundred other television and radio talk shows worldwide.

Her *New York Times* #1 bestselling book, *If Life Is a Game, These Are the Rules: Ten Rules for Being Human*, has been published in more than forty countries. Her books in the Game Rules series include *If Love Is a Game, These Are the Rules; If Success Is a Game, These Are the Rules; If High School Is a Game, Here's How to Break the Rules: A Cutting Edge Guide to Becoming Yourself*; and *The Gift of Motherhood*, and *Baby Boomer's Bible to Life After 50*.

Dr. Carter-Scott's other published works include: *Negaholics: How to Overcome Negativity and Turn Your Life Around; The Corporate Negaholic: How to Deal Successfully with Negative Colleagues, Managers, and Corporations*; and four self-published books and e-books: *The New*

Species: A Vision of the Evolution of the Human Being; The Inner View: A Woman's Daily Journal; and *The Art of Giving: How to Bring More Joy and Pleasure into the Lives of Those You Love;* and published in Holland, *Blij met Mij,* or *Happy with Me!* She lives with her husband, sharing time between Henderson, Nevada; Santa Barbara, California; and the Netherlands.

Lynn U. Stewart is the director of The MMS Worldwide Institute, BV. She not only leads this organization of highly capable team players, but she also develops constituencies in other regions, states, and countries. At the same time, she is a corporate account executive, a professional master coach, a group facilitator, a workshop leader, and she trains and certifies MMS and MMI coachees.

Her corporate specialty is the Employee Owned Change® program designed for businesses who want a bottom-up approach that guarantees "buy in" at all levels of the organization. Her passion for personal growth manifests in The Inner Negotiation Workshops she leads both in the United States and abroad, as well as in the MMS Coach Training, currently offered in the Netherlands.

Some of her corporate clients include: *Better Homes and Gardens* magazine, Burger King, Delco, Unilever, Dole Foods, FMC, GTE, Hyperion Solutions, Marriott Corporation, Montecito Bank and Trust, Orban, Platinum Technology, Paragon Technology, Todd Pipe and Supply, University of California–Santa Barbara, Beverly Clark Collection, Paragon Decision Technology, and Het Expertise Centrum. Lynn lives in the Netherlands.

How to Contact Us

How to Contact Us

Free 30-Day Virtual Training Demo

Go to: www.mmsvt.com/tlc

Enter this Promo Code: drc2008

Enter your information to activate

your 30-day free Virtual Training.

The following is a list of our worldwide representatives and affiliates. They can offer you ways to participate with MMS, through Virtual Coach Training, MMSVT (Virtual Training), live presentations, and licensing opportunities to teach our Coach Training and other courses in your local area.

UNITED STATES

Carol Jones

The MMS Institute, Inc.

P.O. Box 30052

Santa Barbara, CA 93130, USA

Telephone: (800) 321-6342; Outside USA: +1.(805) 683.9353

E-mail: info@themms.com

www.mmsvt.com; www.themms.com; www.negaholics.com

EUROPE
Lynn U. Stewart
Director
The MMS Worldwide Institute, BV
Herengracht 52 N
1016BN Amsterdam

The Netherlands
Telephone: +(31) 650-944740
E-mail: lynn@themms.com
www.themms.eu

NETHERLANDS
A. Nicoline Smoor
licht + ruimte, coaching cn inspiratie
Abcoude
Telephone: +(31) 6 11003354
E-mail: inw-nl@themms.com
www.themms.nl

ASIA
Cindy Yeo
Citadel Consulting Pte Ltd
20A Bali Lane Singapore 189856
Telephone: +(65) 6341 7787 or
+(65) 6341 7747
E-mail: enquiries@citadel.com.sg
www.citadel.com.sg

INDIA
Rahul Gedupudi
Kensium Solutions Pvt. Ltd.
Sahithi Arcade, III Floor
Main Road, S.R. Nagar
Hyderabad, India - 500038
Telephone: +(91) 9949495511
E-mail: rgedupudi@kensium.com
www.kensium.com

AFRICA
Ronell Botha
Operations Manager
ZACRON Empowerment Initiatives
Telephone: +27 (0)11 867-0713
Fax: +27 (0) 86 633 8092
Cell: +27 (0)73 291 0450
E-mail: events@zacron.co.za

MIDDLE EAST
Peter Mayne
Looptech - me FLZ
7th Floor, Fairmont Hotel
Sheikh Zayed Road
Dubai - UAE
Telephone: + 971 4 3124018
Fax: + 971 4 3124019
Cell: + 971506559858
E-mail: peter.mayne@looptechme.com
www.looptechme.com

AUSTRALIA
Kaliope Sikiotis
Telephone: 0061. 41.552.6098
kaliope@people.net.au

SOUTH AMERICA
Otto Driessen
Avenida Teixeira Mendes, 43
Porto Alegre RS 91330-390
Brazil
e-mail: otto.driessen@gmail.com